The

VERY
SHORT
BIBLE

The Condensed Story of the
Old & New Testaments

Condensed, Organized, and Explained by
Dr. Peter J. Bylsma

BYBLIO
PRESS
Inspire, Inform,
and Transform

Byblio Press
11410 NE 124th St., #260
Kirkland, WA 98034 USA
www.bybliopress.com
www.shortbible.com

Ordering Information: This book may be ordered by contacting the
publisher at the address above. Special discounts are available on
quantity purchases by corporations, associations, and others. For details,
contact the publisher at the address above.

The views expressed in this work are solely those of the author and
do not necessarily reflect the views of the publisher, and the publisher
hereby disclaims any responsibility for them.

Maps created by David C. Hoerlein

ISBN: 978-1-964060-00-2 (SC)
ISBN: 978-1-964060-01-9 (eBook)

Library of Congress Control Number: 2024905625

Disclosure

This book is not the Bible. It is a brief and useful summary of the Bible and its main stories and themes, and it has been condensed and explained by the author. After reading this book, readers may want to read the unabridged Bible, or longer summaries of the Bible (*The Short Bible* or *The Simplified Short Bible*), to gain a deeper understanding of the entire story.

CONTENTS

ADDITIONAL MATERIAL

mind and emotions and provides direction to humans about their moral choices. When humans take time to listen and seek direction, communication can occur through insights and a "voice" in the mind. Sometimes communications are more direct – through dreams, visions, or messages from "holy strangers" (angels). On rare occasions, God disrupts the normal laws of nature to intervene directly in human activities, often causing rare natural events to occur at strategic times. These events are called "miracles." Sometimes humans are inspired by the Spirit to speak God's words in extraordinary ways, and believers provide godly advice and rebuke others by using their "spiritual gifts." The Bible itself provides guidance about God's ways and thoughts. Finally, God took on a human form and lived on earth, giving us a concrete example of how we are to live and love others.

Interpreting the Bible can be a challenge. Sometimes the author of a book does not explain what was written because people at that time understood the context. Sometimes specific guidance is written to people in one location at a particular time, and that guidance does not apply to those living in other contexts. Finally, not everything that was written is literally true. Some authors used allegories, metaphors, exaggerations, and parables to convey their messages, and their audiences knew they were not to be taken literally or report historical facts.

Main Themes

The collection of writings has a distinct beginning that moves progressively to a conclusion. No document tells the entire story, but together they have many common themes with a plot that centers on the nature of God and the invisible conflict between the spiritual forces of good and evil in the world. Here are the main unifying themes that run from the beginning to the end.

1. The world has two planes of reality – a physical world that can be seen and measured, and an invisible spiritual world that cannot be measured.

2. Invisible forces have unusual powers. Some forces have good and loving motives, but others have evil motives that destroy what is good.
3. There is only one true and supreme God, which has different forms.
4. There is life after physical death, and the quality of one's life after death depends on God's decision regarding the life a person leads. God's forgiving and gracious nature gives hope that everyone can enter a wonderful life after death.
5. God is good, just, merciful, forgiving, and loving. God wants us to live a fulfilling life and gives us much more than we deserve (grace).
6. God uses people to show the world how life and relationships should look on earth. God first worked through individuals and then through a special tribe of people (the Israelites). Various people reminded the tribe about how they should live, and eventually, people throughout the entire world were chosen to be God's people. These people are to exhibit specific qualities that distinguish them from others – they are to be known by their love for others and by providing justice in society.
7. God wants to have a meaningful relationship with all people without regard to their actions, beliefs, gender, tribe, race, age, or birthplace.
8. There are right and wrong ways to live, things to do and things to avoid. Obedience to God's principles and guidance helps us through life's struggles. Not following these principles may result in severe struggles.
9. God's people often fall away from living the right way. As a result, they suffer the consequences that brings them much pain.
10. Some form of offering or sacrifice is needed to restore a broken relationship. Blood symbolizing life was used in offerings and sacrifices to acknowledge that we fall

short of expectations and that we must forego our own interests to make things right.

11. Life is unpredictable and often unfair. Our plans are interrupted by unexpected events beyond our control. In a world that has both good and evil, good people may suffer and evil people may prosper. Faithfulness to God and our response to our circumstances are what matter the most. God's unlimited love and forgiveness are gifts to all people, even though we don't deserve them.

12. God is very concerned about justice and those who are disadvantaged. God is especially concerned about helping foreigners and the sick, poor, abandoned, despondent, and disenfranchised. Acts of service, compassion, and sacrifice for these groups provide evidence of a God-like disposition.

13. A tension exists in how we live our lives on earth. We are not to conform to the ways of an ungodly world, but we are asked to serve others in that world.

14. God's principles and guidance often contradict prevailing the world's values and priorities. Some biblical teachings are very unusual and not easy to follow.

Contents of This Book

This book has three sections. Part 1 summarizes the Old Testament, with chapter 7 describing unique books that don't fit into a chronological account of the ancient history of God's people. Part 2 summarizes the New Testament. Additional information, including several appendixes, appears at the end of the book.

This book summarizes the main stories and lessons found in the Bible in the order of when the events occurred (the Bible was not organized in chronological order). More information is provided to clarify the text and explain the context and meaning of the stories. Finally, the words of Jesus appear in red text in color versions of this book.

PART 1

THE
OLD TESTAMENT

1
GOD'S PROMISES AND LIFE IN EGYPT

The Beginning

Before time began or anything existed, a multidimensional God was present in the universe. This God was all-powerful, existed everywhere, and knew everything. God's character was entirely good, forgiving, helpful, and kind. God was constantly creating: angels to adore the creator and help in God's work, then light, and then a physical world composed of an extraordinary number of stars and planets. On one unique planet, God created waters and dry lands that eventually yielded living organisms.

Everything was good, but at some point, some angels wanted God's power for themselves and rebelled, causing evil to enter the universe. All that was good now exists alongside corrupt forces that fight what is good.

God then made the most important creation, humans who were unique on the unique planet. God wanted to interact with them, so God gave them some of the same qualities of God – creative, needing to relate to others, able to tell the difference between good and evil, able to love others without any conditions, and willing to put other's interests before their own. The two human "images of God," male and female, were to join together and produce children so the human race would grow. God gave humans (people) the entire planet and all its living things to enjoy. People were to care for the planet and obey certain rules to help them all be self-sustaining and maintain harmony with one another.

Adam and Eve

The first known people were called Adam and Eve and lived in a garden named Eden. They had an abstract relationship with God and a general awareness of what they were to do on earth. Eventually, the leading evil angel known as Satan infiltrated their awareness, and they believed the angel's lies and did not follow the rules God gave them. This disobedience and selfishness infected the human spirit with an invisible disease called "sin" that coexisted with their invisible nature of goodness. Adam and Eve became aware that there were negative consequences when they disobeyed God's rules about how to live.

God allowed evil to exist – eliminating all evil would mean killing all people as well. So we now live in a world where God battles Satan and other evil forces until a time when one side finally wins the war.

Nobody knows when, where, or how all these events happened. What we do know is that (1) a good force created the universe and all things in it, (2) humans make choices that can be either good or evil, and (3) God constantly reveals the benefits of choosing good. God helps people think and act in good ways and sometimes takes direct action to oppose evil in order for people to enjoy a better life and meaningful relationships with God and others. Yet evil forces still exist and want to disrupt the good. Most of the time, the influences of good and evil show up in the actions of individuals, organizations, and the way people live together.

Noah

Adam and Eve eventually had two sons. The older brother (Cain) killed his younger brother (Abel) due to jealousy. After Cain was expelled from the family, the couple had more children, who then had children of their own. Eventually there were thousands of people living on earth.

There was no concrete expression of how people were meant to live, so as the human population grew, life became increasingly violent and corrupt. In fact, there was so much evil in the world that God decided to start the animal kingdoms again. God had Noah, a good man with a good family, build a large ship (an ark) that could house his family and a small number of all the known animal species. When the ship was finished, God caused heavy rains to fall for a very long time. This caused a massive flood and very high waters that drowned all the people and animals that were left behind.

After the rain stopped and the water level fell, plants were exposed and started to grow again. The ship came to rest on high ground, and all the animals and family members left the ark and started reproducing again. Noah made an offering of thanks to a God he didn't know. A rainbow appeared, a sign that God would never destroy all evil on the earth.

Abraham and Sarah

About 4,000 years ago, God decided to create a concrete example to show people how to live on earth. God told a man named Abraham to move his family from Ur (in southwest Iraq) to Canaan, an area now called Palestine. Abraham obeyed God and moved his household 1,000 miles to Canaan. God considered his obedience to be a sign of righteousness (holy living) and changed his name to Abraham; his wife Sarai became Sarah. (See their route in Map 1 in Appendix E.)

God told Abraham that he would lead a tribe of people that was to act in ways that showed others how humans should live in the world. Members of his family and his descendants were to obey God's commands and treat others fairly. God made a promise to Abraham: "I will make you a great nation and will bless you. You will be a blessing, and all the families on earth will be blessed."

God eventually changed the promise to Abraham to a mutual agreement ("covenant"). Abraham's descendants would be very fruitful and rule the region as long as they trusted and obeyed God. As a sign of the agreement, all of Abraham's male descendants had to be circumcised. This also applied to their servants and slaves from other tribes. This would distinguish those who followed their God from all others.

But Sarah wasn't able to get pregnant, which made it impossible for Abraham to have descendants. She told him to have a child with Hagar, their servant from Egypt. Hagar had a boy, and Sarah was very jealous and wanted a child of her own. She treated both Hagar and the boy harshly, causing them to leave home and go into the wilderness. An angel told Hagar that the boy's name was to be Ishmael and that his descendants would settle in the east and also be countless like the stars.

When Sarah was well past childbearing age, an angel told her and Abraham that they would have a child. They both laughed at the idea, but God said a boy would be born in a year and should be named Isaac ("child of promise").

After Isaac was born and while he was still a boy, God tested Abraham's faith by telling him to sacrifice Isaac as an offering on a distant mountain. Abraham and Isaac traveled to the mountain, and as they climbed, Isaac asked his father where the lamb was that would be burned as the offering. Abraham said God would provide the lamb. Abraham built an altar and arranged the wood; then he tied up Isaac and put him on the wood on the altar.

As Abraham was about to kill Isaac, he heard a voice saying, "Do not kill the boy. Since you are willing to kill your only son for me, I know you will obey me." Then Abraham saw a goat in a bush and used it as the offering in place of Isaac. The voice continued: "Because you obeyed me, I will bless you and increase your descendants so they will be like the stars in the sky and the sand on the seashore. Every nation of the earth will be blessed through your descendants."

Isaac and Rebekah

Isaac grew up and married a relative named Rebekah, a beautiful and honest woman who had a gracious spirit and was kind to strangers. Isaac and Rebekah eventually had twin boys. The first baby, Esau, was covered with red hair and was Isaac's favorite child. The second baby, Jacob, had smooth hair and was Rebekah's favorite.

As the two boys grew up, Esau traded the benefits he had as the first born to Jacob in exchange for some food. When Isaac was dying and nearly blind, Rebekah and Jacob tricked him into blessing Jacob instead of Esau. Isaac told Jacob, "May God give you good soil and plenty of grain and wine. May people and nations serve you. Those who bless you will be blessed, and those who curse you will be cursed."

When Esau found out that Jacob had tricked Isaac, Esau was very upset and wanted to kill Jacob, who fled to Haran, a major city about 500 miles north. Jacob had a dream that his descendants would spread in all directions and that through his descendants, all the families of the earth would be blessed. This was the same message God gave both Abraham and Isaac.

Jacob and His Family

Jacob met his cousin Rachel in Haran and wanted to marry her (she was the daughter of Rebekah's brother Laban). Jacob agreed to work for Laban for seven years to pay for her. After working the seven years, Laban told him that he had another daughter, Leah, who was older (and less attractive), and she had to be married first. So Jacob married both Leah and Rachel and worked for Laban another seven years.

Jacob started his family with the two wives. Leah had four sons – Reuben, Simeon, Levi, and Judah. Rachel wasn't able to have any children, which caused more tension between the two wives. Rachel was jealous of Leah and wanted children of her own. She agreed to let Jacob have her maid Bilhah as another wife in order to have children who would be considered her own descendants. Bilhah had two sons, Dan and Naphtali.

As Leah watched Rachel's family grow, she decided to give Jacob her maid, Zilpah, as his wife. Zilpah had two sons, Gad and Asher. Then Leah had two more sons, Issachar and Zebulun, and a daughter Dinah. Finally, after all the years of not being able to have a child, Rachel had a surprise pregnancy of her own and gave birth to a son named Joseph.

After Jacob paid off his debt for his two wives, he worked for Laban for six more years and both families prospered. Jacob then returned to Canaan with his extended family to take over Isaac's property and run his own business. He had been very successful at raising hundreds of healthy animals and took them with him.

As Jacob traveled toward Canaan, he sent messages to Esau to say he was coming home and would share his wealth with him. Esau went to meet Jacob's caravan and Jacob sent him some animals as gifts to make Esau happy. Jacob expected Esau to still be angry and may want to kill him, but when Esau arrived, the two brothers hugged and cried in each other's arms. Esau returned to his home in Edom and Jacob continued traveling south into Canaan.

Rachel died while giving birth to another son, Benjamin. So Jacob had 12 sons and one daughter: Reuben, Simeon, Levi, Judah, Issachar, Zebulun, Dinah, Dan, Naphtali, Gad, Asher, Joseph, and Benjamin. Jacob also took on the name Israel after fighting with an angel during his trip.

Family Crises and a Move to Egypt

Jacob loved Joseph the most of all his sons and made him a coat with many colors. Joseph would tell Jacob about the bad things his brothers did, and they grew to hate him. When Joseph was sent to check on his brothers who were watching animals far away from home, the brothers threw him in a pit and sold him to traders who were traveling to Egypt. They covered Joseph's coat with animal blood and took it to Jacob, saying he was killed by a wild animal. Jacob became so sad that he cried constantly for weeks.

The traders sold Joseph to Potiphar, the leader of those who guarded the Egyptian king (Pharaoh). Joseph was so smart that Potiphar put him in charge of everything in his house. Joseph was also young and handsome, and Potiphar's wife tried to get him to love her many times, but Joseph resisted. One day when only Joseph and the wife were home, the wife tried to embrace him, but Joseph ran out of the house. To get revenge, the wife told Potiphar that Joseph had attacked her but ran away when she screamed. Potiphar then threw Joseph into prison.

Joseph became a leader in prison. He interpreted the dreams of some of the prisoners, and the events he predicted came true. One prisoner knew the king well and learned all about what happened to Joseph. When the man left prison and returned to serve the king, he told Pharaoh that Joseph could interpret dreams. When Pharaoh had dreams he could not understand, he had Joseph explain them. Joseph said he was merely a spokesman for his God, who was the true interpreter.

Joseph told Pharaoh that the dreams predicted seven years of very good harvests, but then seven years of a severe famine. Joseph suggested that Pharaoh hire somebody wise to create a system to store extra food during the years of abundance so food could be used during the years of famine.

Pharaoh liked the idea and saw that Joseph had God-given wisdom. Pharaoh put Joseph, a foreigner who was only 30 years old at that time, in charge of the entire Egyptian kingdom – only Pharaoh had a higher position. Joseph carried out the plan to store food for the coming famine during the seven years of good harvests. While this happened, Joseph started a family with his Egyptian wife and had two sons, Manasseh and Ephraim.

Famine Brings Israelites to Egypt

The famine affected the entire region and grain was the only thing that grew. Jacob sent 10 of his sons to Egypt to get grain while Benjamin stayed behind. When the brothers arrived, they went to Joseph to buy grain because he was in charge of all food in Egypt. But Joseph's brothers didn't recognize him because he disguised himself when he saw them coming and because they all thought he was dead.

Joseph accused them of being spies and asked them about their family. They said their father and one brother still lived in Canaan. Joseph then sold them grain and gave them supplies to take back to Canaan. But he wanted them to come back with Benjamin the next time they came to Egypt.

Jacob told all of his sons to go to Egypt to buy more grain when it was all gone. They introduced Benjamin to Joseph who was so overcome with emotion that he had to leave the room to hide his tears. He returned and then gave them all an amazing amount of food.

Joseph eventually told his 11 brothers his true identity and said:

> I'm your brother Joseph. You sold me to men going to Egypt. Don't be sad or angry with yourselves; it was God who sent me before you in order to preserve your life. The famine has lasted two years and has five years to go. God sent me before you to preserve you as a remnant on earth and keep you alive. It was not you who sent me here, but God, who made me like a father to Pharaoh and lord of all his household and ruler over all the land of Egypt. Go tell our father that I'm alive and that you shall all live near me here in Egypt.

Jacob brought his entire extended family and all their belongings and animals to Egypt, where they settled in the best land in the delta of the Nile River. Joseph provided food for all the families.

Israelites Suffer in Egypt

The tribe of Jacob and his descendants were called Israelites and spoke the Hebrew language. They prospered and grew in number after Joseph and his brothers died. But a new pharaoh didn't care what Joseph had done and realized the Israelites outnumbered the Egyptians. He decided to make the Israelites slaves and made them work in the fields and build Egypt's cities. When the Israelite population continued to grow, Pharaoh ordered the Egyptian nurses to kill all their baby boys. The Israelites suffered extreme hardships and cried out to their God.

Moses Is Born, Then Talks to God

One Israelite family had a baby boy during that time. They were afraid the Egyptians would kill him, so they put him in a basket and pushed it into the plants growing by the shore of the Nile River.

Pharaoh's daughter saw the basket and retrieved it. She realized it held an Israelite baby, and she adopted him as her own child, giving him the name Moses. When Moses got older, he found out he was adopted and who his real mother and father were. He loved the Israelites and was upset that they were treated harshly. When he killed an Egyptian who was beating an Israelite worker, he had to leave Egypt when Pharaoh found out what happened.

Moses traveled to a wilderness region several hundred miles away and started a family. As he worked as a shepherd, an angel appeared to him in a bush that was on fire at the foot of a mountain. But the fire didn't burn the bush, and a voice came from the bush.

> Moses! Don't come any closer. Take off your sandals because you are on holy ground. I am the God of Abraham, Isaac, and Jacob. I have seen the pain of my people in Egypt and have heard their cries. I will send you to Pharaoh so you will bring my people out of Egypt. I will be with you, and when you have brought them out of Egypt, you shall worship God at this

mountain. Tell Israel's leaders that the Lord appeared to you and is concerned about what is being done to them in Egypt. I will bring you all out of slavery and lead you to Canaan, a land flowing with milk and honey.

When Moses was unsure about his ability to take on this task, God gave him some unusual powers and showed him what he was able to do. For example, he could use a long wooden staff to perform various miracles. Since Moses wasn't a good speaker, his brother Aaron would help communicate God's messages to the Israelites and Pharaoh.

Moses Liberates the Israelites

The two brothers returned to Egypt and explained to the Israelite leaders what happened. Moses performed some miracles to prove that God was with him. The people believed him and were glad to know God was concerned about them.

Moses then showed Pharaoh God's powers, and Aaron told Pharaoh, "The God of Israel says 'Let my people go so they can worship me in the wilderness.'" But the king didn't let them go – he couldn't afford to have so many workers leave.

Pharaoh made the Israelites work even harder, and the Israelite supervisors were mad at Moses for coming back and making their work harder. When Moses told the people again that the Lord promised to deliver them from Egypt, they didn't believe him.

Moses and Aaron told Pharaoh many times to let the Israelites leave and showed Pharaoh God's power in some form of affliction that hurt only the Egyptians. Each time an affliction occurred, Pharaoh agreed to let them leave, and Moses made the affliction stop. But each time when things got better, Pharaoh changed his mind and refused to let the Israelites leave.

One last affliction convinced Pharaoh to let them go. God told Moses to have all the Israelites kill a young and perfect lamb at twilight, then spread the lamb's blood above the door and on the doorposts of their homes. At midnight, God caused all firstborn children and cattle to die, but the Israelites avoided this punishment because the blood was a sign to God that the angel of death should pass over the family living inside. The people were to eat a special "Passover" meal that night and celebrate this again to remember what God had done.

And that night, in every household in Egypt except for the Israelites, the firstborn of the family and livestock died, innocent casualties of the ongoing war between good and evil.

Pharaoh was so upset that he ordered all the Israelites and their livestock to leave Egypt as fast as they could. All the Israelites and some of their slaves left Egypt. The descendants of Jacob had been in Egypt for more than 400 years, and now they were heading back to Canaan.

Moses Leads the People in the Wilderness

Moses led the Israelites south toward the Red Sea. They followed pillars of clouds during the day and pillars of fire at night. They soon arrived at the edge of a large body of water. Pharaoh was angry that his slave laborers were gone and wanted them back. He sent his army on chariots and horses to kill and capture the Israelites.

God told Moses to have the people start walking toward the water and to lift his wooden staff and hand over the sea to divide the water so everybody could cross. A strong wind separated the waters and the people walked to the other side. The Egyptians chased the Israelites using the same path, but after all the Israelites arrived on the other side, Moses raised his staff and hand over the waters again, stopping the wind. The water quickly returned to its normal level and rose quickly around the entire Egyptian army. Every Egyptian soldier and horse drowned.

The people were stunned by God's power and believed Moses. They celebrated their victory and honored God who had freed them and conquered their enemy.

2
LIFE IN THE WILDERNESS AND CANAAN

Life for the Israelites in the wilderness was difficult. They couldn't find enough water to drink, but God supplied water in miraculous ways. They were attacked by soldiers of another tribe, but Joshua led the Israelites to victory. The land was getting rocky and could not produce food. When the people complained about being hungry and wanted the food they ate in Egypt, God had a sweet cracker-like substance (manna, or "bread") appear on the ground in the morning like frost and had birds ("meat") fall from the sky at night. The bread would only last one day. On the sixth day of the week, there would be twice as much on the ground, and when it was cooked, it would last two days. Moses told the people that God wanted them to cook what remained from the sixth day and not do any work on the seventh (last) day of the week. This established the tradition of the "sabbath," one day of rest at the end of the week.

When the Israelites camped at the foot of Mount Sinai, God made an agreement with the people. God told Moses, "Tell those in the house of Jacob and his sons: 'You saw what I did to the Egyptians. If you obey my commands and laws, then you will be my people. You shall be a holy nation to me, and I will keep you safe and healthy.'" Moses told the people what God had said, and the people agreed to obey.

The Major Commands and Other Laws

God then came down to Mount Sinai in a fiery smoke, and Moses climbed the mountain to meet God, who said, "I am the Lord your God, who brought you out of Egypt and slavery. I am a jealous God, but I will show my love to those who love me and keep my commands." Then God gave 10 commands to Moses.

(1) I am to be your only God. (2) Do not make an idol or anything looking like a god, and do not worship or serve them. (3) Do not use or say my name carelessly – treat it with great respect. (4) Remember the sabbath day – keep it holy. Do all your work in six days, but on the seventh day, nobody in your household, including your animals and visitors, shall do any work. (5) Honor your father and your mother so you may live a long life. (6) Do not murder. (7) Do not commit adultery. (8) Do not steal. (9) Do not lie against others. (10) Do not desire anything that belongs to your neighbor.

In addition to these 10 commands, God told Moses about many laws the people must follow. Most related to providing justice and making sure people live the right way. There were laws about owning slaves (if a person buys an Israelite slave, the slave must go free on the seventh year without any more payment). There were laws about personal injuries (a person who kills or kidnaps another person shall be put to death; if there is a fight, the penalty is equal to what happened – a life for a life, an eye for an eye, a tooth for a tooth). There were laws about property rights and relationships (anybody who makes a sacrifice to another god will be destroyed; don't treat strangers badly, for you were strangers in Egypt). There were laws about money (if you lend money to the poor, do not charge interest; give a tithe (10%) of everything from the land to the Lord). And there were laws about justice and correct living (if you meet your enemy's animal wandering away, you must return it to him; do not take a bribe; be nice to foreigners).

God told Moses that an angel would guard them as they traveled toward Canaan. If the people obeyed God, they would defeat those who tried to stop them. They weren't to keep anything related to the gods of the tribes they conquered. They would control a vast region and keep it only for themselves because letting other tribes live among them would damage their way of life and love for God.

Moses told the people what God said, and they agreed to follow God's commands and laws. Moses wrote down all the things God told him in order to preserve the commands and laws as reminders for future generations. An ornate box (the Ark of the Covenant) was built to store sacred items that were collected along the way to Canaan.

Israelites Abandon God

When Moses and Joshua went up the mountain again and did not return for 40 days, the people thought they had died and built a golden statue of a calf as a god—they worshipped the calf and made sacrifices to it.

When Moses returned, he was extremely angry when he saw the golden calf and the people dancing around it. He had the golden calf burned to the ground, and Moses told the Levites to kill the men who rebelled (they were going to cause trouble while they traveled to Canaan).

God was also extremely angry, calling the people very stubborn in their resistance to change, and wanted to destroy them all. But Moses reminded God of the promise to make them a great nation. God reconsidered and told Moses to continue leading everybody toward Canaan.

To make God's presence more visible, a tabernacle where God would live was built using contributions from the people. Detailed instructions described how priests should make sacrifices and how worship should occur. Aaron became the High Priest and his sons were also priests. When the tabernacle was finished, ceremonies were held to bless the priests who would work in it. When the ceremonies ended, a cloud covered the tent in the tabernacle and God filled it. The God who had delivered and saved Israel was finally living with the chosen people.

More Rules for Living

God spent several more months providing Moses with many rules about how the priests were to conduct their religious affairs, how people were to worship, and how Israelites – as the people of God – were to live as a community. Some of the rules were specific while others were general principles. God was holy, and the Israelites had been chosen to be a holy people, God's representatives on earth to show others how to live and glorify God. But since humans will always sin in some way, the people were to stand before God and repent, making sacrifices and burning offerings to show their sorrow and be cleansed of their sins. Offerings and sacrifices made in the tabernacle had to be high quality, using the finest grain and animals without any defects, which symbolized perfection.

Shedding blood was key in the sacrifice to mend a broken relationship between God and humans. Through sacrifices and offerings, God forgave the people, separating them from their sins, and restoring the relationship between God and humans. Related to this idea was a special Day of Atonement that was to be observed once a year. It involved sacrificing one goat and having the High Priest put his hands on the head of another goat, confessing all the people's sins, and transferring the people's sins into that goat. This second goat was then released into the wilderness to symbolize that the people's sins were removed (a "scapegoat").

Moses gave detailed instructions about what to eat and not eat, what could be touched and not touched. The instructions were practical and helped maintain the people's health. For example, anyone with a skin disease had to be quarantined and practice social distancing from others – they had to move out of the camp, wear torn clothes, not comb their hair, and yell, "Unclean! unclean!" to others until they were healthy. New washing methods had to be followed, which were quite advanced for that time; when followed, these methods gave the Israelites an advantage in battle and helped them live longer.

Some rules dealt with the principles of morality and justice. For example, there were rules and penalties associated with specific crimes, and people were commanded to "love your neighbor as yourself." The rich and poor were both to be judged in the same way. Foreigners were to be accepted and loved just like everybody else, just as the Egyptians had welcomed the Israelites during the famine. A field was not to be harvested to its edge, and the poor and foreigners were allowed to eat the food at the edge as well as anything that fell to the ground during the first harvest. A sabbath year was established that was similar to the weekly sabbath day. In the seventh year, land was not to be tilled, and the food coming from it was freely available to anybody who wanted it. And every 50 years, the Year of Jubilee was celebrated – the possessions of the poor that had been sold so the poor could survive had to be returned to the original owners.

The rules and instructions ended with reminders of the consequences of how people live. There are many rewards and blessings for those who obey God's laws and commands, but punishment occurs when people do not obey. If the nation of Israel breaks its agreement with God, it would lose their land, be scattered across the region, and become the slaves of its enemies. Yet even after people disobey, there is forgiveness and reconciliation when the people are sorry and apologize and start obeying God again. There is no permanent condemnation for those who disobey God – there is always a way to earn the benefits of the agreement again. God's nature is forgiving and extravagant when it comes to being in a relationship with humans, the most valued creation.

Lack of Faith Extends the Journey to Canaan

One year after leaving Egypt, the people celebrated the Passover, then started their journey toward Canaan (about 250 miles north). God was in the tabernacle, and when the cloud rose from the tabernacle, the Israelites moved on. Priests used trumpets made from animal horns to announce meetings, signal the time to move forward, prepare for battle, and celebrate offerings during their festivals.

After traveling 30 miles, some of the people started complaining about the food. They dreamed of the food they had in Egypt and were tired of eating the same food every day. God was upset with their attitude, and Moses thought his job was too difficult. God told Moses to gather 70 men around his tent, and the Spirit filled them so they would also become wise and help lead the people.

As the Israelites approached Canaan, God told Moses to have one man from each of the 12 tribes travel into Canaan to gather information about who was living there and what kind of food was being grown. The 12 spies scouted the region thoroughly and reported back that the land was excellent. But they also said the people were strong and would be very hard to defeat in battle. Ten spies said that occupying Canaan would be impossible, but two spies, Caleb and Joshua, said that God will give them the victory if the Israelites continue to obey God.

The 10 doubters convinced the leaders that a successful invasion was impossible, and the people were angry with Moses and Aaron because they had led them on a meaningless trip. They wanted to kill Caleb and Joshua and replace Moses with a leader who would take them back to Egypt.

God was very upset with the Israelites, but Moses argued with God and said God's reputation as a power that was "slow to anger, full of love, and forgiving our sin and rebellion" would be spoiled if God abandoned the Israelites. Moses asked God to forgive the sins of these people, just as God had done in the past.

The Lord agreed to forgive the Israelites, but said nobody who was at least 20 years old, other than Caleb and Joshua, would enter Canaan. They would all need to wander in the wilderness for 40 years, one year for every day the spies explored the land.

Moses then led the people into the desert back toward the Red Sea. The 10 spies who stirred up the crowd caught a plague and died. After seeing that these spies died and facing 40 more years of wandering in the wilderness, the people repented. But many of their confessions were not genuine; they only repented so their trip to Canaan would resume. Moses told them that they had to stay together and all go back into the desert, and that God would not be with anybody who left the group. Some of them insisted on moving north on their own to invade Canaan, but when they did, they were defeated.

There were rebellions against Moses while the Israelites lived and traveled through the wilderness. His authority was challenged and the people often complained about the food, the lack of water, and their living conditions. But eventually they resumed their trip toward Canaan. They defeated different enemies they met along the way. Eventually they took over the land on the east side of the Salt Sea and camped east of the Jordan River across from Jericho, a large walled city in Canaan.

Final Words from Moses

By this time, Moses was very old and nearing death. God gave him specific instructions about what the people should do when they entered Canaan.

> When you cross the Jordan into Canaan, drive out all its inhabitants, destroy all their images and idols of their gods, and demolish all their altars. Occupy and settle in the land, for I have given it to you. If you don't drive them out, those who remain will be stumbling blocks for you – they will give you trouble, and then I will do to you what I plan to do to them.

Moses summarized the main events that had occurred during the previous 40 years and stressed how important it was to honor God, keep the commandments, and obey the rules that were established – all of them were from God. Moses also warned the people about the consequences of not being faithful. He knew their major challenge would be spiritual in nature. He told them:

If you become corrupt and do evil, God will be angry
and you will quickly perish from the land. The Lord
will scatter you among other nations, and only a few
of you will survive. But if you then seek the Lord
with all your heart and soul, you will find God. Later
you will return to the Lord, who is merciful and who
will not abandon you or forget the promises made
with your ancestors. Hear, O Israel: The Lord our
God is one Lord. You must love the Lord your God
with all your heart, with all your soul, and with all
your strength. You will be blessed if you listen to my
commandments, but you will be cursed if you do not
listen to them and turn away from me.

Moses gave more instructions about what should
happen when Israelites entered Canaan. God would lead
them to victory over the larger and stronger nations, and
these nations must be totally destroyed. The Israelites were
not to make treaties with the other nations and were not to
show them any mercy. They were not to intermarry with the
families of other nations because it would lead the Israelites
to follow other gods. Anything related to another god had
to be destroyed.

To keep the Israelites from getting arrogant about their
success, Moses told them, "It is not because you are righteous
or good that you will take possession of their land. Rather,
it's because of the wickedness of these nations. After all,
God considers us a stiff-necked people." The people were
to love and obey God, not in a formal and routine way, but
because God had first shown love for the Israelites in many
ways. Love was at the heart of the relationship.

After Moses died, God chose Joshua to become the new
leader of the Israelites, and he told the people to prepare to
cross the Jordan River and enter Canaan. (See the route of
their entire journey in Map 2 in Appendix E.)

The Israelites Conquer Canaan

Many different "nations" of people lived in Canaan. They
did not get along with each other, and many of the cities

had strong walls. Their leaders believed in many gods that the people thought demanded horrible things. For example, it was common for the people to think their gods wanted children to be killed as a sacrifice.

Joshua sent two spies across the river to learn more about Jericho, the first city they would battle. They met a sinful woman named Rahab who informed them that everybody in Canaan already knew about the Israelites and their powerful God and planned to take over the region. Everybody was very afraid of them.

City guards saw the spies as they visited Rahab and went to her house and told her to release them. But she hid them on her roof and told the guards they were no longer there. The guards believed her and left to look for them. Rahab asked the spies to spare her and her family from the coming destruction – she had saved them and wanted to be saved as well. The spies devised a plan to ensure she did not die when the city was attacked. She then helped the spies escape the city, and they made their way back to Joshua across the river.

The next morning, Joshua ordered the Israelites to gather at the Jordan River, which was at the flood stage in the spring. After the priests put their feet in the water, the river stopped flowing. (A huge section of rock had just broken off a hillside 15 miles upstream, causing a reservoir to form and stopping the flow of the river.) The people then crossed the river and camped close to Jericho.

Rather than attack, the Lord told Joshua to have the entire army march around the city once a day for six days. Priests led the parade and played their trumpets with the army trailing behind. The army was silent as they marched. On the seventh day, they marched around the city seven times, and when the army heard one long blast of the trumpets, they all gave a loud shout. The walls of the city collapsed and the army rushed into the unprotected city and killed everybody except Rahab and her family members, who were all allowed to live with the Israelites. Joshua then burned Jericho to the ground.

Joshua Attacks the South and North

Word spread quickly in the region about what happened to Jericho. The different kings that controlled the land in Canaan knew Israel's god was much stronger than theirs, and they lost the courage to fight.

The Israelites attacked many other cities in the region. The nearby kings combined their armies so they would fight against Israelites as one army, but the Israelite army defeated all of them. Joshua and the army conquered all the cities south of Jericho and left no survivors.

Then he and the army turned north. The nations in northern Canaan heard what happened to the armies in central and southern Canaan and banded together to fight Israel's army. But in a surprise attack, the Israelite army routed the combined forces of the opposing armies, and then it defeated the massive chariot-led army of the large city of Hazor and burned it to the ground. Israel's army then pursued the retreating armies of the northern nations all the way to Phoenicia. Everybody was killed, but other than Hazor, no city was destroyed, for they would be used by the Israelites in the future. The Israelites kept all the livestock and valuables from the people for themselves. This ended all the fighting.

It took seven years for Joshua to finish all the battles, and 31 kingdoms had been conquered in Canaan. The battles and cleansing of Canaan were meant to eliminate the powers of evil in the region, demonstrate to the world the power of Israel's God, and create a society of holy people who didn't compromise with evil. But some areas were not occupied, so people from other tribes still lived in the region. Joshua had essentially done what God and Moses had told him to do – eliminate Canaan's inhabitants who had cold hearts against the one true God. This allowed the Israelites to settle in the promised land, but they still coexisted with nonbelievers.

Joshua gave land to the 12 tribes of Israel according to the number of people in each tribe: larger tribes inherited more land. The Levites were given 48 towns to live in within the land of each tribe and land outside these towns for their animals.[1] Six towns inherited by the tribe of Levi were designated to be "safe refuges" so people could seek safety if they accidentally killed somebody. (See the areas of the 12 tribes in Map 3 in Appendix E.)

---

[1] The 12 tribes that inherited land were Reuben, Simeon, Judah, Issachar, Zebulun, Benjamin, Dan, Naphtali, Gad, Asher, and Joseph's two sons, Ephraim and Manasseh.

3
ISRAEL'S STRUGGLES AND LEADERS

Because of the distances and a lack of unity among the 12 tribes, there was no place for tribal leaders to make decisions or determine how to work together. As a result, each tribe developed its own ways for living in the area where they settled.

The tribes fought battles with those who were still living in the region. Several major cities were still controlled by the Canaanites because the Israelites in their area were not strong enough to defeat them in battle. In some cases, the local people rebuilt cities the Israelites had destroyed and became powerful again. Some Israelites became friends with the Canaanites and adopted their ways of living, including taking part in religious ceremonies to other gods. Intermarriage led to further decay of the people's faithfulness to God's commands and religious rituals. Moses had warned the people about not doing these things, and the people had promised not to do them. But most people did whatever they wanted to do.

Over the next few centuries, there was a consistent pattern of behavior among the Israelites. They would start out honoring God, but they would get comfortable, conform to the ways of the local customs and culture, and gradually forget to follow God. This resulted in oppression by others which led the people to experience the absence of God's blessings. When things got really bad, the Israelites would appeal to God for help, and different heroes emerged to defeat the oppressors. Their victories were due to God's power, not the power of Israel's armies. It was through human weakness and limitations that God's power and glory were revealed. God continued to be faithful and forgive those who called out for help, obeyed the rules for good living, and had faith. The victories restored peace and justice until the cycle of decline started again.

Israelite Leaders

Gideon and Jephthah

Gideon was one of the faithful leaders. God told him that he would be a mighty warrior, but he doubted this was possible. He had no training, was from a small village in the weakest tribe, and was the youngest in his family. He wanted a sign to prove that God was with him. Several miracles occurred to prove to Gideon that God had chosen him to lead the army and would be victorious. He had more than 32,000 men in his army, but God told him that was too many – if he won the battle, people would not give credit to God. Through a series of tests to reduce the number of men in the army, Gideon ended up with only 300 men. With such a small army, if Gideon won a battle against all odds, only God would get the credit.

Gideon's men launched a surprise attack during the night, which caused panic among the enemy and caused them to fight and kill each other. Gideon's men chased those who retreated for many miles beyond the Jordan River. More than 135,000 enemy soldiers were killed in this long battle. The victory brought the Israelites 40 years of peace.

After Gideon died and several decades of peace, the Israelites started worshipping the local god, Baal, and other gods again. Foreign powers took over the region and mistreated the Israelites.

After 18 years of domination by the Ammonites in the east, the Israelites asked Jephthah to lead an army to fight this enemy. He was an illegitimate son who was mistreated by his half-brothers and had run away from home. He lived with homeless men at the edge of the desert and became famous as a fearless warrior who led a gang of bandits. The Israelite leaders said they would make him their leader if he defeated this enemy.

Jephthah agreed and first tried to negotiate a peaceful solution with the enemy king about a land dispute, but that effort failed. Jephthah then went and destroyed 20 of the enemy's cities and led all of Israel for six years until he died.

Samson and the Philistines

Eventually the Israelites turned from the Lord again and followed foreign gods. The Philistines, a strong tribe that occupied land on the Mediterranean Sea, dominated the region and controlled Canaan for 40 years.

An Israelite couple who lived near Philistine territory had a son named Samson who was to be a Nazarite from birth – he would not consume any form of a grape, not touch a dead person, and not cut any hair on his head. Samson became famous for his great strength, but he was also impulsive and quick-tempered and lacked wisdom and good moral character. For example, he slept with strange women, married foreigners, and often broke his vow not to touch a dead body. He killed thousands of Philistines because of his bravery and great strength, and he ruled over Israel for 20 years.

Late in his reign, Samson fell in love with a woman named Delilah. The Philistines asked her to find out why he was so strong, and they paid her to find out his secret. Delilah asked Samson several times how he got so strong. Each time he lied about it, and each time Delilah told the Philistines what he had said. When the Philistines tried to capture him, he fought them off because he was still strong.

Delilah complained many times to Samson about how he had lied to her. She said he didn't love her and made her look like a fool. She nagged him about it daily until he got sick of her nagging and told her the truth: his strength would go away if his hair was cut. Delilah told the Philistines this secret, and after she cut off his hair while he slept, God left him and the Philistines easily captured him. They gouged out his eyes and made him a prisoner and forced him to grind grain.

Eventually his hair grew longer and he regained his strength. When the Philistine rulers took Samson out of prison to make fun of him for a very large crowd, he had his handler put him between two pillars that held up the building so he could lean on them.

Samson then prayed, "Please Lord, remember me. Strengthen me one more time and let me get revenge on the Philistines for my two eyes." Then Samson pushed against the pillars with all his might, and the temple collapsed and killed everybody in it.

Ruth and Boaz

During these troubled times, migrations occurred because of fighting, famine, and family unification. During one famine, a small family that lived in Bethlehem moved beyond the Salt Sea. The husband died and left behind his wife Naomi and two sons. The sons married Orpah and Ruth, two local women. When the sons died, all that was left was Naomi and her two daughters-in-law.

Naomi heard that God had provided food in Judah, and she wanted to go back home. Ruth insisted on going with her and said, "Where you go, I will go; where you live, I will live. Your people will be my people, your God will be my God. Where you die, I will die." She was committing herself to the ways of the Israelites.

When Naomi and Ruth arrived in Bethlehem, Ruth worked in the barley fields that belonged to Boaz, a wealthy landowner who was related to Naomi's dead husband. Boaz saw Ruth was a hard worker and told her to work for him. Ruth bowed to Boaz and asked him, "Why have you noticed me and liked me, even though I am a foreigner?"

Boaz replied, "I've been told what you have done for your mother-in-law after your husband died and how you left your parents and homeland to live here with people you don't know. May the God of Israel reward you."

Boaz gave Ruth food to take home and made Ruth feel welcomed. Ruth continued working for Boaz, and eventually they got married and had a son named Obed, who later became the father of Jesse, who had a son named David, who would become Israel's greatest leader.

Samuel, the Prophet and Judge

A childless woman named Hannah desperately wanted a child and made a vow to God: "If you give me a son, I will give him to you for all the days of his life." God answered her prayer: she had a son and named him Samuel. He worked and lived in the tabernacle as a boy and took his duties seriously. He eventually became a judge and religious leader. He liberated cities the Philistines had captured, and there was peace between Israel and its neighbors while Samuel was the leader.

Crowning a Unifying King

The different Israelite tribes fought among themselves and sometimes were angry when they were left out of battles where they would have gained something from a victory. During these civil wars, the people of the various tribes stole from each other, including taking women from other tribes to be their wives. The tribes felt no loyalty to one another and were jealous of each other. There was no king, and each tribe acted in its own self interests.

Without a unifying king and a way to select the next king, the tribes of Israel had little prestige in the region. The Philistines posed the biggest threat to Israel, and there were enemies to the north and east. Having the sea on their western border was not an advantage because Israel had no expertise with sailing. They were surrounded by trouble and needed to defend themselves, but the 12 tribes were not working together in any way to do so. Religious life was mostly neglected, and the priests took advantage of those who came to the tabernacle to worship and make sacrifices.

Saul, Israel's First King

When Samuel was old, he was asked to appoint a king to lead the nation. The people wanted to be like the other nations that had a king. Samuel said that having a king would mean the Israelites would have to spend a lot of money and time and hire many people to serve the king and protect the kingdom. But they didn't listen – they wanted a king to be like other nations.

God told Samuel to appoint a king and that the next day, a man would come to town from the tribe of Benjamin (the smallest and least prestigious of all 12 tribes) who should be Israel's first king. The next day, Samuel met a tall handsome man named Saul who came to town. Samuel privately told Saul that he would become Israel's first king. Samuel blessed him and described things that would take place the next day that would confirm to Saul that he was the chosen one.

Saul became a changed man, and everything happened the next day that Samuel had predicted. God's spirit filled Saul and he spoke the truth clearly. People who knew Saul were amazed at his changed personality.

Saul was 30 years old when he became Israel's first king. Samuel reminded the people that having a king was not going to save them if they did not obey the Lord. Although Saul was tall and handsome, he had personality flaws that ruined his chances for greatness. He was insecure because he came from the smallest tribe, and he was always worrying about what others were thinking of him. It was clear to those on the battlefield that he lacked confidence in his military strategies. He lacked good judgment when dealing with others, was suspicious of others' motives, was jealous when others received recognition, and set up monuments to honor himself.

But worst of all, Saul disobeyed God. He got scared and offered sacrifices when it looked like he might lose a battle. Before one important battle, Samuel told Saul that God wanted him to completely destroy the enemy and all their possessions. However, after winning the battle, Saul spared their king, and his soldiers persuaded him to let them keep the best animals. When Samuel met Saul after the battle, Saul said that everything had been destroyed. But Samuel knew this wasn't true – he heard the sounds of sheep and cattle in the background.

Samuel was furious and said, "Does the Lord delight in your offerings and sacrifices more than obeying God? Rebellion is sin and being proud is evil. Because you rejected the Lord's word, God has rejected you as king." Samuel never talked to Saul again.

David Rises, Saul Falls

Samuel mourned Israel's condition and went to Bethlehem to meet with Jesse, the grandson of Boaz and Ruth, to identify the next king. Jesse brought seven of his sons to Samuel, who rejected all of them. They were physically impressive, but God told Samuel not to look at their outward appearance. "The Lord looks at the heart."

Samuel asked if there were any others, and the youngest was out tending sheep. David was called to the room, very healthy and handsome. Samuel said David was to be the next king. David was a good speaker, a brave warrior, a musician, and a poet. When Saul was tormented by evil spirits, David played a small harp to sooth and comfort Saul. David visited Saul many times while being a shepherd of his family's flocks.

Goliath

When the Philistines threatened to raid Israel again, the two armies stood opposite each other on the hills above a valley. The Philistine army had a soldier named Goliath who was nearly seven feet tall. He had heavy armor and weapons, which were perfect for hand-to-hand combat. However, he was slow and visually impaired, so he could be killed by somebody who used a different method.

Goliath went into the valley each day for more than a month and challenged Israel to send one soldier into the valley to meet him in a winner-take-all fight. Saul and his entire army were terrified and nobody volunteered to fight Goliath.

Several of Jesse's sons were with Saul at the battle site, but David was home tending sheep. Jesse had him take food to his brothers, and when David arrived, he found out about Goliath's challenge. David volunteered to fight Goliath, but Saul said he had no chance against such a large and experienced warrior.

David told Saul, "I've been caring for my father's sheep, and when a lion or bear attacks a sheep, I kill it. If I can kill a lion or bear, I can surely kill Goliath. He has defied the armies of the living God."

Saul agreed to let David fight Goliath. Saul put his heavy armor on David, but David said he couldn't fight that way. Instead, he would use the weapons he used as a shepherd: a wooden staff, a few smooth stones, and a sling. The stones, whipped fast and released by the sling, could travel at more than 100 miles an hour and were very lethal in the hands of a skilled slinger, even from hundreds of feet away. With God on his side and a lethal weapon in his hand, he went into the valley with confidence to fight Goliath.

When Goliath saw how small David was and that he had no armor, he mocked and cursed him. But David told him, "You fight me with a sword and spear, but I fight you in the name of the Lord Almighty, the God of the armies of Israel, whom you defy. So now the Lord will deliver you into my hands. I will cut off your head, and the entire world will know there is a God in Israel."

As Goliath moved closer for the attack, David ran forward, put one stone in his sling, and shot it directly at the giant. The stone hit Goliath in the forehead and knocked him to the ground. David ran up, grabbed Goliath's sword, and cut off the giant's head, lifting it for all to see. When the Philistines saw Goliath was dead, they turned and ran. The Israelite army chased them and killed them as they went.

Saul Pursues David

David became very famous and was very successful when he went into battle. Saul was jealous of David's fame and got increasingly paranoid. He tried to kill David several times and had his men chase him around the region. David always escaped and even had several chances to kill Saul, but each time he chose not to because Saul had been appointed king by God. David knew that if he was to be the king, he shouldn't make the process go faster by disobeying God's command not to murder — God's process would allow him to become king the right way. David hid in different locations and eventually moved to Philistine territory for safety where he was out of Saul's reach.

Saul and his sons were eventually killed in a battle with the Philistines. He received no royal burial, and with their victory, the Philistines controlled all of Canaan.

David and Solomon, Israel's Greatest Leaders

When David heard of Israel's defeat and Saul's death, he knew it was his time to become king. He was crowned the new king in Hebron, but one of Saul's sons was crowned as the next king by other tribes. The families of both men had disputes for several years about who was the right king. Through a series of negotiations and fights between those backing each man during this civil war, David emerged as the king when he was 30 years old.

David Rules and Israel Expands

David soon attacked and defeated the foreign powers that occupied Jerusalem, and the city became known as the City of David (also referred to as Zion because of a hill in the city with that name). The city became the nation's political and religious capital, and with the help of the Phoenicians, a large palace was built to be David's home. He danced in the streets of Jerusalem when the Ark of the Covenant came into the city. David had many wives and many other women who all produced many children. God told David through the prophet Nathan, "I will make your name great. I will raise up your offspring to succeed you, and I will establish his kingdom. Your house and kingdom will endure forever."

David's armies defeated the Philistines several times as well as enemies in the southeast. He pressed far northward past Damascus and eastward to occupy more territory. The Lord gave David victories wherever he went, and he always gave God the credit for the military victories and material prosperity as the empire expanded.

David and Bathsheba

David experienced a significant scandal when he saw a beautiful young woman named Bathsheba bathing near his palace. She was married to a soldier who was far away at a battle. David had an affair with her and she got pregnant. After David arranged to have her husband killed in battle, he married Bathsheba and their baby was born.

David thought he had committed the perfect crime. Nobody knew the full story, but God knew. The prophet Nathan told David a story about a rich man who stole from a poor man. David was angry with the rich man and said he must die. Then Nathan said to David:

> You are the rich man! The God of Israel says to you, "I anointed you the king of Israel and saved you from Saul. I gave you all of Israel and Judah. Why did you do evil? Now the sword will never leave your house and your family will be affected by evil."

David realized that he had sinned against God. Nathan said that the Lord had forgiven him, but the baby would die soon after it was born. The baby died a week after it was born. Later, the couple had another baby boy and named him Solomon.

David was a lenient father and there was strife within his family and throughout the empire for many years. As Nathan had predicted, immorality and rebellion grew, and there was much bloodshed within Israel and within his family.

David eventually made plans to build an elaborate Temple, and at the end of his reign, he held a public meeting to recognize Solomon as his successor (he was not yet 30 years old). David is still known as Israel's greatest leader, even though he and many others suffered because of his sins.

King Solomon and the Temple

Solomon was king during a time of peace and prosperity. His most important accomplishment was building a permanent Temple that was the center for religious worship of Israel. Up until then, the tabernacle used tents for worship. The Phoenicians provided skilled architects and technicians to design the Temple that conformed to the plans for the tabernacle laid out by Moses. The Temple was huge and took up twice the amount of land that the tents of the tabernacle required. For example, the Temple entrance had huge pillars made of bronze, 24 feet high and 18 feet around. Its huge doors had inlaid gold and elaborate decorations that opened into the sanctuary, which had well-decorated floors and walls. No stone could be seen on the inside.

It took seven years to complete the Temple, and when it was finished, the people were so happy that they sacrificed thousands of animals at its dedication to show their gratefulness to God.

Solomon's Wisdom and Wealth

Solomon was known for being a wise king who knew how to deal with complex and unusual cases. He prayed to God for wisdom, and he got it. In one case, two women came to him, both claiming to be the mother of a child. Solomon said he would cut the child in half and give each woman part of the child. Hearing that, one mother said she would give up the child to the other, thereby showing that she was the true mother. People from all over the world came to Solomon to learn from him.

Solomon's wisdom and excellent organizational skills kept Israel at peace with its neighbors and helped make the nation wealthy. The growing wealth of the people trickled upward as they paid heavy taxes, and with the gifts from many visitors, Solomon was the wealthiest king in the world.

Solomon had many wives, including women from other nations. Despite Moses's warning not to marry foreigners, he married the daughter of the Egyptian pharaoh and women from five of the nations on Israel's borders to help ensure peace. He pushed Israel's empire further than David had and met women with different value systems and beliefs, which Solomon tolerated in the spirit of being flexible. His harem had 700 wives and princesses and another 300 women that produced children for him. Success and prosperity tainted his judgment, and he gradually compromised his values and acquired idols of worship and built altars to worship gods associated with his many wives.

Near the end of Solomon's reign, adversaries rose up around the kingdom and challenged his rule. Threats also came from within. Jeroboam was one of Solomon's officials and met a prophet who told him that Israel would be divided into two parts after Solomon died and that Jeroboam would be the leader of one part of the kingdom.

Solomon reigned for 40 years and was replaced by his son Rehoboam. His reputation as a wise ruler endures to this day, but many of his accomplishments depended on the slave-like labor of the Israelites who were taxed heavily to make Israel great. It had been nearly 500 years since Moses led the Israelites out of Egypt and set up the tabernacle in the wilderness. Now Israel was a nation like others, with a king and a permanent place to worship. Like David, Solomon's legacy was a mix of greatness and personal failures.

(Map 4 in Appendix E shows the areas controlled by the three kings.)

4
EVIL KINGS RESIST PROPHETS' WARNINGS IN A DIVIDED KINGDOM

When Solomon died, two men thought they should be king. As Solomon's successor, Rehoboam was crowned king by the tribes of Israel. However, some leaders complained that they wanted relief from the low wages and heavy taxes Solomon put on them. They wanted Jeroboam to be the king. When Rehoboam decided not to reduce the taxes and demanded even more from the people, those from all the tribes except Judah walked out and made Jeroboam their king.

The nation was on the brink of a civil war. But war was averted when a prophet said God wanted the tribes to split into two kingdoms. Those in the tribes of Judah and Benjamin were in the south, and they called themselves *Judah*. It was known as the *Southern Kingdom* and included the capital in Jerusalem. Those from the 10 other tribes in the north called themselves *Israel*, and their "nation" was known as the *Northern Kingdom*. (Map 5 in Appendix E shows the areas of the two kingdoms.)

The two nations were rivals and often battled in the many years that followed. The border between the kingdoms was about 10 miles north of Jerusalem. Both nations had 20 kings, and their division reduced each kingdom's power. As a result, they were often attacked by foreign invaders. Various prophets spoke and wrote to both nations when their people strayed from God's ways.

The Northern Kingdom and Its Prophets

Jeroboam changed the ways religion was practiced in the north. He set up golden calves as their god and appointed priests who had no experience carrying out their duties. Anybody could be a priest, and it was an easy job with many benefits. Jeroboam's reign as king lasted 22 years. He resisted prophets who condemned his evil decisions.

Of the 20 kings that served in the North, a few had very long reigns (one ruled for 41 years), and some were very short (one lasted just 7 days). Nearly all the kings were evil. Many prophets spoke God's truth to the kings about the need to turn from wicked ways, but the prophets were usually ignored or killed.

Amos, Elijah, Elisha, and Hosea

Amos was a prophet during Jeroboam's reign. The region was experiencing easy living during a time of prosperity, but wealth was not distributed evenly and many social injustices existed. Through selfish luxury and the oppression of the poor, the wealthy lived well while many others struggled.

Amos wrote that religious rituals are meaningless when a lack of fairness exists. He criticized social injustice in other nations and in the Southern Kingdom and said divine judgment would come to them. But then he wrote that the same things were happening in the Northern Kingdom: social evils, injustice, and immorality. If others deserved punishment, so did Israel. In fact, it was even worse because the Israelites were God's chosen people and should know better. The wealthy people of Israel hated accountability, resisted the truth, accepted bribes, neglected the poor, and harassed the righteous. Amos said their punishment would be inevitable and predicted an exile – God could not be bribed with offerings and sacrifices when the people's sinfulness prevailed. But he also predicted the Israelites would return from exile and experience a time of peace and that David's dynasty would continue through a remnant of people who stayed faithful.

Elijah was the main prophet who spoke God's truth in the Northern Kingdom. After Elijah predicted a drought, he hid in the desert and then lived with a very poor widow north of Canaan. The king's men were sent to kill him, and they killed other prophets, but they couldn't find Elijah.

He eventually emerged and told the king that the drought occurred because Israel didn't follow God. Elijah challenged 850 prophets of Baal and other gods to a test of power; he would be God's only prophet. The prophets of Baal failed in their attempts to have Baal burn a sacrificed bull, even after they danced and prayed for many hours. Elijah taunted them: "Shout louder. Surely Baal is a god! Maybe he's deep in thought, or busy, or traveling. Maybe he's sleeping." The prophets shouted louder and cut themselves, tore down Elijah's alter, and prayed frantically, but nothing happened.

Then Elijah rebuilt his altar, dug a trench around it, and had the king's prophets pour water on the bull so it was totally soaked and water filled the trench. Then Elijah prayed, "God of Abraham, Isaac, and Israel, let everybody know you are God and I am your servant." Fire fell from the sky and burned the bull, the alter, the soil, and consumed all the water in the trench.

Everybody who watched fell and cried, "Your Lord is God!" Elijah told them to kill all the prophets of Baal, and soon heavy rains started that ended the 40-month drought. He continued to speak truth to the Northern Kingdom, and he blessed Elisha as the next prophet. Elijah was taken into the sky in a tornado right before Elisha's eyes; a large search party spent three days looking for the body, but no body was found.

Elisha performed many miracles among the people. In one case, a Syrian working for Israel's army named Naaman had a noticeable skin disease. He had married an Israelite woman who told him about Elisha's miracles of healing. He met Elisha who told him to wash in the Jordan River seven times. Naaman got upset at this demand, but his servants told him that if Elisha had asked him to do some great act that used his strength to be healed, he would surely do it. Was he too proud to wash in the river? So Naaman humbled himself and washed in the river, and he was healed.

Israel and Syria battled occasionally and the Northern Kingdom gradually lost land. By using his God-given insight, Elisha often advised Israel's leaders of the Syrian plans, so Israel was always prepared for their attacks. The Syrian king thought there was a traitor in their midst, but he was told that Elisha could predict the future and knew about the attacks in advance.

The Syrian king wanted Elisha dead and surrounded the city where Elisha was staying. But Elisha was not afraid because God sent a multitude of horses and chariots burning with fire in the hills. When the Syrians approached the city, God blinded them. Elisha then told their leaders that they were attacking the wrong city and he would lead them to where they would find who they were looking for. Elisha led the blind army to Samaria where Israel's king and army were located. When God opened their eyes, they were surrounded by their enemies!

Elisha told the king to feed the Syrian army and send them home. The Syrians returned home and stopped their raids into Israel for many years. When the Syrian attacks resumed, they surrounded Samaria and stopped food from entering the city, causing a famine in the city. But God provided food the next day when the Syrians fled after hearing thunder-like sounds resembling a charging army with chariots. The people of Samaria then had access to all the food and animals the Syrian army left behind.

Hosea was one of the last prophets to warn Israel of its coming doom. Using poetry, he wrote that God asked him to take a prostitute as his wife and produce children with her. That way he would understand how God feels when dealing with an unfaithful partner. The names of his children indicated that Israel was like somebody who was unfaithful in a marriage because they had fallen in love with other gods. Therefore, God would leave them because they had committed adultery. Hosea was warning Israel that they would be cut off from God's protection and their palaces and fortified cities would be destroyed. God desires mercy and recognition, not sacrifices and burnt offerings. "Israel must return to God, maintain love and justice, and always wait for God." Hosea ended his message like Amos, who previously predicted God would still love them the way parents love their children. God forgives and heals the faithful, and some would return and live in the land God had given them.

The Southern Kingdom and Its Prophets

Like the kings in the north, many of the kings of Judah were unfaithful to God. There were longer periods of peace and prosperity in the Southern Kingdom than in the north and longer periods when these descendants of David and Solomon listened to God's prophets and stopped worshiping other gods. Some of the faithful who lived in the north defected and moved into the Southern Kingdom – Jerusalem was still respected and was close to the border. Of the 20 kings of Judah, Manasseh was king the longest (55 years), while several others were king for only three months.

Like those who lived in the North, those living in Judah did evil in the sight of the Lord. Under Rehoboam, the first king, people set up many altars to other gods and did the same awful things that were done by those who originally lived in Canaan. Egypt attacked Jerusalem and took away all the gold items that Solomon had put in the Temple and royal palace.

Just as prophets spoke and wrote to the leaders and people in the north and made predictions about events to come, various prophets spoke and wrote in the same ways to those in the Southern Kingdom.

Jehoshaphat, Isaiah, and Micah

Jehoshaphat was a king who reigned 25 years. He made reforms that returned the people to the religious practices used under David and Solomon. He had altars to foreign gods removed, and his good policies brought peace between Judah and the Philistines and Arab nations. He also had good relations with the Northern Kingdom, so Judah didn't have any enemies on its borders. These religious and political policies led to peace and economic prosperity in the Southern Kingdom. When he was rebuked by a prophet, he listened and made reforms. For example, he installed judges who emphasized fairness and did not take bribes.

Yet Jehoshaphat didn't listen to every prophet when he was confronted, and some of his ways were passed on to his son Jehoram when they ruled together. When Jehoram took full control of the throne, Judah fell back into idol worship and experienced wars again. Jehoram murdered six of his brothers and built altars to idols. His only son Ahaziah continued the horrible rule of his father.

Isaiah wrote the most of all the prophets and predicted a coming king. He was born during prosperous times, and his extensive poetry and other writings harshly condemned Israel's steady moral decline due to corruption and unrighteousness. But he also provided great hope in things to come in the future. Judgment and hope are woven throughout his words, which were written over many years.

He first wrote that God condemns those in Judah and Jerusalem because they are corrupt and full of evil ways. Their sacrifices and religious gatherings are meaningless because the people don't obey God. Through Isaiah, God said,

> Do you think I want all these sacrifices and offerings? I'm disgusted by the smell of your incense. When you raise your hands in prayer, I don't see you; when you say many prayers to me, I'm not listening. Stop doing evil! You have not been fair to others, you have not helped those who suffer because of your unfairness, and you have not supported orphans and widows.

Israel was like God's vineyard, and if it didn't produce fruit despite the owner's many efforts, the vineyard would be destroyed. In real life, the godless nations of the Assyrians and Babylonians would be the destroyers, used by God to punish the Israelites.

Isaiah also provided hope for restoration. Although the Israelites would be defeated and destroyed, correct living would lead to peace for those who trusted God. Eventually the conquering evil nations would be overthrown, and out of what remained of the Israelites that survived, a descendant of David would come to power and lead a worldwide kingdom that would last forever. Evil would be destroyed and God's vineyard would be fruitful once again.

Isaiah wrote about a righteous leader to come, Immanuel ("God with us") who would be "Mighty God" in human form and prevail throughout the entire world. God says: "People will be judged based on their justice, fairness, and correct living." However, judgment and destruction will come first. Those who have faith don't need to worry because the "grains of wheat will be separated from their chaff." Their hope is in what comes after their struggles, and those who wait will be blessed, for God gives strength to those who are tired and weak. "Those who have hope in the Lord will renew their strength. They will soar high like eagles, they will run and won't be weary, they will walk and won't faint."

Isaiah described the one to come as a "servant." Abraham was God's first servant because he obeyed the call to move to Canaan. Israel was a nation chosen by God to be an obedient servant and a witness to the world of God's power and compassion. The coming servant would have God's spirit so his kingdom will establish justice that extends to other nations (non-Israelites called "Gentiles").

The coming servant would be innocent and live correctly. He will be like a shepherd who tenderly cares for his young sheep. He will look like a normal human being but would be very special in other ways – the only one of his kind to walk the earth. Yet he would be misunderstood and rejected by many people, and he would be killed in a gruesome manner. Yet through the sacrifice of his own blood, this servant would save all people from their sins, bringing all people to God, even those who are not part of the nation of Israel. He would later be raised and praised.

These unusual messages are intertwined. A person of great power and goodness would be rejected by those he comes to serve. He would not use his power or reason to defend or save himself, and his death brings life to others. He would go into hell, conquer death, and come back more powerful than ever, and he will give others some of his great powers. The servant is the greatest of all!

Isaiah wrote about the coming king to the tribes of both kingdoms who had become blind, deaf, and disobedient. He wrote that God says:

> I am doing something new! I'm making a road through the wilderness and will lead the blind in ways they have not known. I will turn darkness into light, so don't be afraid! You are mine, and when you pass through the waters, I will be with you. When you walk through the fires of life, you won't be burned. The coming king will be despised, rejected, and suffer. He will take on our pain and be killed for our sins. His punishment will bring us peace. Even though he was never violent and never lied, he won't protest. But he will know what is happening. It's God's will for him to be crushed, for his life is an offering for our sin, and he will intervene for everybody who sins.

Isaiah continued writing about judgment. He knows what God requires and doesn't see it among the people. He appeals to the people and leaders to turn away from violence, idol worship, and being unfair to those who lack power. He calls people to return to the Lord. God says:

> You have your religious rituals and practice fasting and praying, but you don't treat others fairly. Do you expect me to listen to your prayers, be impressed, and bless you? Your rituals occur once a week. What I want is for you to have a humble spirit and to offer encouragement and support to those with broken hearts. I'm pleased when I see my people breaking the chains of injustice, releasing people from the heavy yokes that are on them, feeding the hungry,

giving shelter to the homeless, clothing the naked, and supporting those who lack power – these are signs of true religion. When I see these things, I will hear you and heal you, and light will come to your darkness.

Isaiah says that God sees nobody who meets the definition of holiness, and he concludes with a description of the signs that indicate the coming king, the Redeemer, has arrived. The Redeemer will say:

The Spirit of the Lord is on me and has anointed me to proclaim good news to the poor. God has sent me to comfort the brokenhearted, to free captives and release prisoners from their darkness, to proclaim the Year of Jubilee, to comfort all who mourn and grieve, to give them a crown of beauty instead of ashes, and a garment of praise instead of a spirit of despair.

Isaiah said the peace-creating ruler of this revived kingdom would be a descendant of David. The ruler's kingdom would grow and dominate the world, bring peace, influence other nations, and triumph over the godless. Isaiah writes:

In the last days, nations will go to the Lord together and learn how to work with each other in the right way. God will be the judge between people and will settle the disputes nations have with each other. Nations won't fight with each other, and their people won't train to wage war anymore. They will change their swords into plows and their spears into pruning hooks.

Micah wrote at the same time as Isaiah and Hosea with messages of judgment and hope. He saw the political and religious corruption in the region, and his strong criticism was similar to what Isaiah and Hosea wrote. He said both Jerusalem and Samaria (the main cities in the south and north) were evil because of their idolatry, their corruption that oppressed the poor and ignored justice in the courts, and their general lack of interest in solving society's problems. King Solomon had written wise proverbs about how laziness caused people's poverty, but Micah writes that people may also be poor because those with power ignore the problems of the poor and use all their privileges to maintain their extravagant lifestyle.

But unlike Amos, Isaiah, and Hosea, Micah doesn't tell the Israelites to repent. Instead, he calls them to "court" to make their case before God, who is both the witness and the judge. What does God require for people to escape possible punishment? People are to "act fairly, love kindness, and walk humbly with God." Moses said people should love God and their neighbor as themselves, and the people had not done that. Therefore, the people will lose in God's court because they didn't have the right relationship with God and others. The penalty for their misbehavior was the destruction of their nations and cities, and they would be hauled away in exile to Assyria and Babylon.

After predicting judgment and exile, Micah provided hope for the future. A small number of weak and exiled Israelites would return and build the cities again. "God does not stay angry forever but delights when people show mercy." Micah also predicted that Israel's future leader would come from the town of Bethlehem.

* * * * *

The Israelites in the north and south didn't listen to the prophets' warnings and predictions of the coming invasions by their enemies. Injustice, violence, and religious sinfulness continued in both Israel and Judah, and their leaders didn't realize how soon the prophets' predictions would come true. (Map 6 in Appendix E shows more details about of the two kingdoms.)

5
BOTH KINGDOMS FALL

The Assyrians often attacked areas occupied by the Israelites, Syrians, and Phoenicians. One Assyrian king was particularly brutal as he expanded towards the Mediterranean Sea, and he started taking captives back to Assyria instead of letting conquered peoples stay in their land. Outsiders were brought into areas where the local people had lived, and Assyrian officials supervised the land. This reduced the chances that people would rebel.

When the Assyrians first attacked areas in the Northern Kingdom, Israel's kings would give them money, food, and other things to buy peace. Eventually, the Assyrian army conquered all areas in the region except for the hills in central Canaan. The Assyrians captured more than 27,000 of Israel's political and military leaders and took them back to Persia and Mesopotamia. The Assyrians replaced them with their own people, and the mix of people from many areas and cultures outside Israel resulted in many different types of religious practices. Nobody followed the Lord, and all the cultures intermarried with each other. Collectively, they were known as Samaritans because the capital city had been Samaria.

The Northern Kingdom ceased to exist in 722 BC. The kingdom had lasted about 210 years after splitting off from those living in Judah. In the final 30 years, Israel had six kings and was in rapid decline. Their collapse was predicted by the prophets, but their leaders never appealed to God for help. They had forgotten how obedience to God had made them great.

The South Survives but Ignores the Prophets

People and leaders in the Southern Kingdom continued its evil religious practices, but Judah's strategy to deal with Assyria was different. Judah's leaders depended on political strategies to maintain their prosperity and peace. They cooperated with the Assyrians who invaded the surrounding areas and defeated the Philistines as its army moved toward the prized Egyptian empire. The prophet's predictions about the fall of the Northern Kingdom had come true, but the leaders in the South did not listen to the prophets' warnings. When one prophet warned the people of Judah that they wouldn't prosper if they continued to disobey God's commands, he was killed in the Temple. Some leaders were faithful to God, but most did not obey God and abused their power.

Hezekiah, Josiah, and Jeremiah

Hezekiah was a faithful king who abolished idol worship, smashed altars to false gods, cleansed the Temple, and started celebrating Passover again. He invited the Israelites in the north to take part in these activities. Twenty years after the Northern Kingdom fell, he gave the king of Assyria 11 tons of gold from the Temple as payment for peace and the withdrawal from cities in Judah that had been captured.

But when Hezekiah died, his son Manasseh took over as king and led Judah into its worst period of wickedness. Altars to Baal were rebuilt and practices associated with strong evil powers were commonplace, including human sacrifices, awful sexual practices, and demon worship. The prophets who condemned these practices were killed (Isaiah was probably one of them). Hezekiah had led Judah to its highest point of morality, but his son led Judah to its lowest point.

Hezekiah's grandson **Josiah** became king when he was only eight years old. Judah had kept the peace by making treaties with other nations, paying the Assyrians, and sometimes benefiting from God's powers. Judah gained more independence when the Assyrians started pulling out of the region. Judah also expanded its influence among the northern tribes, which renewed a sense of national pride among all the Israelites. By the time Josiah was 16 years old, he had stopped worshipping false gods and was honoring the true God. Later he started another round of religious reforms and removed priests who led idol worship. When he read the original book of the Law written by Moses in the Temple's rubble, he was disgusted with how far the Israelites had fallen away from God and the Law.

During this period, **Jeremiah** spoke to the people and leaders of Judah and said that Jerusalem's fate would be the same as that of Israel a century earlier – destruction and exile. He knew people would not like what he would say, but he knew God would support and protect him through difficult times and keep him out of trouble. God told him, "I chose you before I formed you in the womb; I appointed you to be a prophet to the nations." Jeremiah told God that he didn't speak well and was too young to be a prophet, but God said, "Don't say you are too young. You must go everywhere I send you and say what I tell you to say. Don't be afraid – I will be with you and will rescue you."

Jeremiah knew Josiah and supported his reforms. When Judah's next set of kings returned to idol worship, Jeremiah warned them about the coming disasters of defeat and exile. The people and leaders persecuted him – he was arrested, beaten, imprisoned, and threatened with death many times. At one point, Jeremiah was thrown into a waterless well to starve slowly in the mud, but he was pulled out by a team of men who used a long rope made of rags. False prophets said Jeremiah's predictions wouldn't come true and that people should ignore his messages of judgment and the need to repent.

Jeremiah's messages also contained hope. A small number of God's people would return from foreign lands, and God would create a new agreement with them that replaced the original agreement made with Moses and the Israelites. In this new agreement, God's laws would be written on the hearts of all people, and all their sins would be forgiven. A descendant of David would emerge and install justice and right living on earth, and their land would never again be overthrown.

Joel, Zephaniah, Nahum, and Habakkuk

Other prophets to Judah spoke similar messages: God will judge the people for their disobedience, they should repent because God is merciful and forgiving, those who don't repent and obey will be destroyed and taken away, but there is hope for those who love God and survive. These prophets included **Joel**, who wrote that God has a Spirit that is available to all people without regard to their age, gender, or social status. As the only universal God who has authority over all creatures on earth, God would eventually judge all nations. Those opposing God will be defeated, but the faithful will be victorious.

The prophet **Zephaniah** shocked the proud and satisfied people of Judah by writing that God's judgment would come soon. He predicted that Jerusalem would be destroyed and its people would be captured and taken to Mesopotamia as their punishment. He said the people should accept this fate and submit to the foreign invaders. People were to be humble, repent, and live the right way. If God punished other nations for their godless behavior, surely God would punish the Israelites for doing the same thing.

The prophet **Nahum** wrote poetry that condemned the Assyrians for their oppression, cruelty, and wickedness. While God is "slow to anger and a refuge for those who trust the Lord, God will not leave the guilty unpunished." Any nation built on sinful living and cruelty will eventually fall. God's kingdom, which is based on fairness for all and correct living, will triumph. God is the Lord of all nations and controls their future.

The prophet **Habakkuk** wrote about a conversation he had with God rather than address the people of Judah directly. The faithful wondered why those who were unfair to others were not punished. God replied that something highly unusual would happen – the evil Babylonians would be used by God to punish Judah. Habakkuk then asked why God would use evil to punish evil. God replied that eventually the Babylonians would be conquered themselves and God's people would rise again. Meanwhile, "the righteous will live by their faithfulness." Being faithful means being dependent on God, not simply following laws and rules.

The Southern Kingdom Falls

The Assyrians eventually lost their power to the Babylonians, which used their power against Judah as they pushed south to conquer Egypt. At one point 10,000 leaders of Jerusalem were captured and sent to Babylon. Any hope of a revived Israel crumbled as Judah was gradually torn apart and its kings did what foreign nations wanted them to do. Jeremiah continually told Judah's King Zedekiah to surrender to the Babylonians to avoid bloodshed, but he didn't surrender. Jeremiah had wept for many years about the stubborn Israelites and how they ignored his messages of God's judgment and need to repent. He probably wrote the book of poetry called **Lamentations** which describes what happened when the Babylonians destroyed Judah and the people's sadness when Jerusalem and the Temple were destroyed.

Jerusalem was captured by the Babylonians in 586 BC after being surrounded for more than two years. The city was burned to the ground and its walls were torn apart. The poorest of the survivors stayed behind and tried hard to stay alive, and Jeremiah stayed with them. The survivors were attacked by nomads from the east and lost their homes. Eventually, most of them decided to go to Egypt to be safe, and Jeremiah probably went with them.

* * * * *

The Southern Kingdom lasted 136 years longer than the Northern Kingdom. The descendants of Abraham and Sarah who moved to Canaan were known as Jews, a term derived from the tribe and nation of Judah. The term was later applied to all Israelites, regardless of their tribe or nation. Their religion was known as Judaism, and they had a unique culture. Jewish people have a shared sense of nationhood and an identity as God's chosen people. The area known as Canaan, from the Mediterranean Sea to the Jordan River, is also called Palestine and the Holy Land. But few Jews lived in the area after both kingdoms were defeated, and most of them were sent hundreds of miles to the east or moved elsewhere. (Map 7 in Appendix E shows where the Jews went after being conquered.)

The Israelites kept good records of historical events and important people who lived in Canaan, migrated to Egypt, wandered in the wilderness, conquered Canaan, and lived in Palestine. But when Jerusalem was raided and most of the Jews were taken to Babylonia, good record-keeping stopped. As a result, we don't know much about the lives of those living in foreign lands.

The land the Israelites left behind was controlled by the Edomites and Babylonians. The Jews had left slavery in Egypt, defeated local powers in Canaan, and withstood stronger nations of Syria, Assyria, and Babylonia. But due to their disobedience to God, in about 500 years the Jews went from having their first king to having no king at all. By the time Jerusalem was conquered, it had been more than 1,250 years since Abraham moved to Canaan, and now most of the Jews were in Mesopotamia, hundreds of miles from the home of their ancestors in Canaan. Palestine mainly became a battleground between the Egyptians and Babylonians.

6
LIFE IN EXILE,
THEN RESTORATION

Eventually the Babylonians were conquered by the Persians led by Cyrus the Great. The Jews living in the region were usually treated kindly, and they learned the language of Aramaic, which was used in business, trade, and diplomacy. Most of the Jews became active in the local economy. Some worked on construction projects – they had experience building large structures in Palestine. Some worked in agriculture and others became involved in business and trade. A few worked in government affairs. They tried to live together in cities scattered across the region so they could maintain their customs and religion.

The Jews who lived in Babylonia wondered when they would return. False prophets predicted they would return soon, and this led to rebellions against the Babylonians because they thought God would free them. But the rebel leaders were executed. Meanwhile, Jeremiah wrote letters from Palestine to those who were in exile to say they should settle down and accept their punishment from God. He told them to "build and live in houses, plant gardens, take wives and have children, seek the welfare of the city where God sent you, and pray to God for the city, for in its welfare you will find your welfare." His predictions that they would return one day gave them hope – they just had to be patient for the right time to go. That confused those living in exile: were they going home soon or not?

Ezekiel and Daniel

The prophet **Ezekiel** was a well-educated and religious Jew who lived in Babylon. When he was 30, God called him to speak to the Jews who lived in Babylonia about when they would return to Palestine. He had a very unusual vision from God, and he used symbolic riddles, stories, and actions to dash the hopes of the Jews who wanted to return to Jerusalem. He had predicted that the Jews in Jerusalem would be captured, and he said those in exile would not return home in the near future – with the collapse of Jerusalem, there was no place to go.

Ezekiel communicated in unusual ways. He acted so strangely that the Jews in Babylon visited him to see his weird behavior. His visions had the message that the Jews would return to their homeland. He said God's reputation throughout the world would be restored and Israel would be one nation again. He had a vision of dry bones lying in a field that came back to life and were joined together and then covered with skin to be alive again. He explained what God wanted them to know:

> It is not for your sake that I'm doing these things, but for the sake of my holy name, which you have harmed among the nations. I will show that my name is holy. The nations will know I am the Lord. I will give you a new heart and put my spirit in you. There will be one king over all of you, one shepherd.

Daniel and His Faithful Companions

Daniel was both a religious leader and a political leader who lived in Babylon before Jerusalem was destroyed. He was trained well in religious activities when he lived in Judah, and he was very bright and wise. He became fluent in Aramaic because he and three other Jews (Shadrach, Meshach, and Abednego) were invited by King Nebuchadnezzar to learn Aramaic when they arrived in Babylon. Daniel wrote messages in both Hebrew and Aramaic, which made his messages available to non-Jews in other nations.

When he and his three friends were given unclean food during their training, they refused to eat it. They asked to receive just vegetables and water, and in 10 days they were healthier than those who ate from the royal menu. After three years of training, the king saw that the four men were far superior to all the others who served him.

When the king had a disturbing dream and none of his magicians and astrologers could tell him what he had dreamt and what it meant, he ordered all the wise men in Babylon killed. When Daniel was about to be taken away, he asked why he was being killed. When he heard about the king's order, he asked to talk to the king after he had a chance to hear about the dream. Daniel explained the situation to his three companions. They all prayed hard to God for insight into the dream.

Daniel then had a dream that revealed the answers to the king's questions. In the morning, he told the king, "Nobody on earth can answer these questions, but there is a God in heaven who knows the meaning of your dreams. This God has revealed to me that it describes what will happen in the future." Daniel then explained to the king what the dream was and what it meant. The end of the dream revealed that God would establish a kingdom that would never be destroyed.

Daniel had answered correctly. King Nebuchadnezzar honored Daniel and his God, saying, "Surely your God is the God of gods, the Lord of kings, and a revealer of mysteries." The king then made Daniel the ruler over the entire province of Babylon and put him in charge of all its wise men. Daniel arranged to have the king appoint his three friends to supervise all the government's work of Babylon.

Later during his reign, King Nebuchadnezzar made a 90-foot golden statue of himself in a field near Babylon. At its dedication, everybody was ordered to bow down and worship it; those who didn't would be thrown into a furnace of fire. Daniel's three friends were at the dedication but didn't bow down, and it was obvious to everybody that they disobeyed this order. The three men were arrested and taken to the enraged king. The men told the king, "We don't need to defend ourselves to you. If you throw us in the fire, our God can deliver us from it. But even if our God doesn't save us, we want you to know that we won't worship another god or bow to the golden image you set up."

The king was furious and ordered them tied up and thrown into the furnace. Its heat was so hot that the soldiers who took the men to the furnace were killed by the flames. But the three men did not burn in the furnace, and those watching saw four figures walking around in the fire – God was with them. The king ordered them to come out of the furnace, and when the three men emerged, they had not suffered any burns. The king was so amazed that he issued an order that nobody should say anything bad about the God of the Jews, and anybody who did would be killed. The king then promoted the three men.

When the Persians conquered Babylon, Daniel continued working as a leader in the Persian government. Others were jealous of his power and plotted against him, but Daniel's reputation as a wise and fair government official was flawless. Two officials plotted to have Daniel punished because of his religion. They got the king to issue an edict that anybody found worshiping a god other than the king during the next 30 days would be thrown into a pit with lions. When the officials found Daniel praying toward Jerusalem in his usual way, they told the king.

The king was dismayed because Daniel was such a highly respected person. But the officials reminded the king that he had issued an edict that couldn't be changed, so Daniel was thrown to the lions. The king told Daniel, "May your God, whom you always serve, rescue you!"

The den was sealed with a large stone and the king couldn't sleep that night. In the morning, the king went to the pit and called Daniel's name. Daniel replied, "My God sent an angel who shut the mouths of the lions. They have not hurt me because God found me innocent." The king then had Daniel removed from the pit and had the men who plotted against Daniel thrown into the pit, along with their wives and children. They all were quickly killed and eaten by the hungry lions.

When Daniel was very old, he had strange dreams and visions about what would happen in the future. He wrote that many evil kingdoms would rise, and many holy people would be killed. But these earthly kingdoms would someday be destroyed forever by a final kingdom, set up by God, that will not end. Although he didn't understand the meaning of these visions, he wrote them down so others could read them later when their meaning could be determined.

A New Policy Prompts Their Return and Restoration

Persia's King Cyrus reversed the policy of moving people from areas he conquered back to Mesopotamia. He encouraged people who had been captured to return home and worship their own gods, and he allowed Jews to return home. But by that time, many of them had settled into well-paying jobs and were living comfortably, and they ignored the opportunity to move to Palestine.

King Cyrus believed in the Jewish God and wanted to rebuild the Temple in Jerusalem. He encouraged Jews in Babylonia to give gold, animals, and supplies to those who wanted to return home and rebuild the city and Temple. About 50,000 Jews soon made the 900-mile journey back to Palestine, and Cyrus sent articles that had been taken from the Temple. When they arrived, it had been about 70 years since the first set of exiles from Judah arrived in Babylonia. (Jeremiah predicted there would be 70 years of exile.)

Jerusalem had been deserted for 50 years and was in ruins. It took the Jews seven months to get organized and start practicing their religious activities again. They made burnt offerings and celebrated their festivals. Construction of a new Temple began using materials purchased from the Phoenicians, and the Levites supervised the work. While many celebrated their return and praised God, the elderly who remembered what Jerusalem had looked like cried openly and bitterly at the shape it was in.

Those living in nearby Samaria wanted to help build the Temple. The Samaritans occupied land in what had been the Northern Kingdom and had intermarried with the foreigners who were brought to the region. When they were not allowed to help, they were mad at the returned Jews and worked against their efforts to rebuild the area. Work on the Temple stopped for 16 years because of their opposition.

Haggai and Zechariah

Work on the Temple resumed when King Cyrus was replaced by a new king in Persia who was interested in the religion of his empire. The prophet **Haggai** reminded the people that building the Temple was a higher priority than making their own nice houses even better. Construction on the Temple soon started again, but their enthusiasm for the project weakened when they realized the new structure would not come close to what had been built under King Solomon. Although they lacked the workers and money to do the job right, Haggai encouraged the people by predicting the new Temple would be greater than the previous one. God spoke through Haggai.

> Be strong, for I am with you. My Spirit remains among you. In a little while, I will shake all nations, and what is desired by all nations will come, and the house will be full of glory. The glory will be more than in the previous house.

At the same time, the prophet **Zechariah** had a similar but longer message for the Jews. In a series of symbolic dreams, visions, and messages, he sees that God's people have returned and their nation is gradually restored. When the Temple is built, the people are promised a glorious future. Although Judah had fallen, Jerusalem will rise again while all the other nations will fall. The Lord said "Jerusalem won't have walls because so many people and animals will live in it." God would rebuke evil (Satan) and a servant leader called the Branch would lead the restoration. This leader will be a priest before God and remove the sins of all people in a single day. Justice and peace will replace wickedness, and God's spirit will spread out across the world. All these things will happen if the people obey God – it is not enough for them to fast and pray. The Lord spoke through Zechariah:

> Provide true justice. Show mercy and compassion to one another. Don't be mean to widows, the homeless, the foreigner, or the poor. Don't plot evil against each other. Those who came before you didn't listen, and they were scattered and became strangers in other nations. So speak the truth to each other and make fair judgments in your courts.

Zechariah also made predictions about the future. A humble and good king would enter Jerusalem riding on a young donkey. Weapons of war would be removed, and peace will come to earth. Many types of people and powerful nations will tell each other about this king. "They will grab you and ask to go with you because they know God is with you." But Zechariah ended with a warning: Jerusalem will be destroyed again and many people will leave the region because the Jews reject the shepherd who came to save them. But after a massive crisis, God will return and rule the entire world.

Encouraged by these two prophets and a hope for a glorious future, the people completed the Temple five years after construction restarted. It was built on the same site as the previous Temple, but it was not nearly as nice. Yet the Jews began their religious activities using the same instructions provided by Moses. The Israelites who had stayed in Palestine joined them in their religious ceremonies and festivals.

Esther and Mordecai in Persia

Many Jews decided to stay in areas controlled by the Persians. When the queen of the Persian King Xerxes disobeyed a direct order in Susa, the king decided she should be replaced. Young women throughout the empire were brought to the king so he could select a new queen. Each woman went through a year of beauty treatment before seeing Xerxes.

Esther was among those brought to see the king. She was a young and faithful Jew who also lived in Susa. She had been adopted by her older cousin Mordecai because her parents died. When she met the king, she impressed him so much that she was chosen to be the next queen. But Mordecai told her not to say she was adopted or a Jew.

When Mordecai overheard a conversation about a plot to kill the king, he reported it to Esther, who told the king, saying she heard it from a man named Mordecai. When the king learned the plot was true, he executed the conspirators.

The prime minister, Haman, ordered everybody to bow to him when they saw him, but Mordecai refused to do it. Haman found out that Mordecai was a Jew, so he devised a plan to get rid of all the Jews in the kingdom (about two million people). He told King Xerxes, "There is a group of people scattered across your kingdom who keep themselves separate from others. Their customs are different and they don't obey your laws. It's not good for you to have them live this way. If you want, you can order them all killed."

The king agreed and issued an order that was sent to every province. It said that all Jews, including women and children, should be killed on a specific day 11 months later. Jews throughout the empire wept and fasted when they heard this order. When Esther found out about the order, she decided to talk to the king. But nobody was allowed to see the king in his private room of the palace unless he invited them in – those who entered without an invitation were killed by his guards.

Mordecai told Esther that it was her duty as a Jewish leader to do something – she might be killed because she was a Jew. Esther told him to have all the Jews in Susa pray for her for three days, and then she would go into the king's private room. She told Mordecai, "If I die, I die."

After three days, Esther went into the king's private room and stood at his door. He invited her into his room, and she was relieved she wasn't arrested or killed. She asked him if she could host a dinner with just him and Haman. He agreed, and as they ate and drank that night, the king asked Esther what she wanted – he would do almost anything for her. She said she would give him her answer the next day when the three of them could eat dinner together again.

That evening, Haman went home and bragged to his wife that he had a private dinner with the king and queen and was going to do it again the next night. But he said he still had a bad day because Mordecai didn't bow down to him. His wife said Mordecai should be killed and hung on a tall pole the next morning before he had dinner. Haman liked the idea and ordered the pole to be set up.

The king couldn't sleep that night. In the morning, he found out Mordecai, the man who reported the assassination plot, was a Jew, but nothing had been done to honor him. When Haman came to talk to the king about killing Mordecai, the king first asked him what should be done for somebody who honors the king. Haman thought the king was going to honor him, so he said the person should put on royal clothes and be featured in a grand parade. The king then told Haman to go and do what he suggested to Mordecai. The humbled Haman did it, and then he returned to have dinner with the king and queen.

As they ate, Esther said her request was for the king to spare the Jews, her people. The king had forgotten who thought of the idea, so he asked who was responsible for the order. She said it was Haman, the man sitting with them!

The king left in a rage, but Haman stayed behind and begged Esther for his life. When the king returned, he saw Haman kneeling at Esther's feet and thought he was trying to assault her. The king ordered his guards to haul Haman away. The guards said there was a tall pole outside of Haman's house that was going to be used to hang Mordecai. The king ordered Haman to be killed and hung on the pole, and the king gave Haman's estate to Esther. When the king found out that Esther and Mordecai were related, he made Mordecai his new prime minister.

But the order to kill all the Jews was still in place. Esther begged the king to issue another order that removed the order to have all Jews killed. The king had Mordecai write the new order, and it was translated into every language spoken in the empire. The order granted Jews in every city the right to protect themselves and kill anybody who attacked a Jew.

The Jews in every province were overjoyed. Their courageous queen and new prime minister had spared them. They celebrated by feasting, and the occasion became known as the days of Purim and is still celebrated by Jews.

Ezra and Nehemiah Return to Jerusalem

A highly educated Jew named Ezra living in Babylon was a Levite and understood all the religious writings that had been handed down through the centuries. He also kept track of everything that happened among the Jews over the centuries. He wanted to return to Jerusalem and got permission from the King Artaxerxes to leave. The king liked the idea of having more Jews return to Palestine and gave Ezra permission to set up a government in Palestine and all the money he needed to reestablish religious systems and buildings, including what he needed for the Temple. The king also said that everybody who worked at the Temple did not have to pay any taxes.

Ezra told the Jews about the planned trip back to Palestine, but not many of them wanted to travel nearly 1,000 miles to a land they didn't know. Many worried about their safety during the trek, and very few Jews decided to return to Palestine. Those who did return traveled safely to Jerusalem.

Ezra soon determined that the Israelites in the region, including the priests, had intermarried with people from other cultures and religions. He was disgusted and angry that they had adopted non-Jewish practices. He told all the Jews about the danger of intermarrying with non-Jews. The people agreed to change their ways, and when Ezra found out that all the priests and Levites had intermarried, they all agreed to cancel their marriage promises.

Nehemiah and Malachi

Many years after Ezra returned to Jerusalem, the city was still being rebuilt. The Temple had been completed but the city walls and gates were still not in place. The city was not a safe place to live. Nehemiah, a highly loyal Jew who worked for the Persian king in Susa, found out that life among the few exiles who returned to Palestine was not good. He wept and prayed for months to determine what God wanted him to do.

Eventually he told King Artaxerxes why he was sad, and he got permission to return and rebuild Jerusalem. He got the supplies he needed and letters from the king to make sure his caravan was treated well and to get free lumber.

When Nehemiah arrived, he saw that the city was not safe and needed to have its walls and gates rebuilt. Everybody agreed to start working immediately on the repairs. He set up a system to guard the gates and gaps in the walls while repairs were made by groups of men from Israel's different tribes.

Those living in the area felt threatened by a stronger city controlled by the Jews, and they plotted to attack the city. Nehemiah increased the security around the city, and everybody contributed what they could. His enemies kept trying new ways to trick him into doing something wrong, but Nehemiah wisely managed each situation and avoided getting in trouble with the king.

The wall and gates were completed in 52 days. All the people in the region were impressed with the strength of the Jews and their God, and it restored respect and prestige to the Jewish nation among those living in the region. Jews from the countryside filled open areas of the city, and people felt secure in the rebuilt city.

Nehemiah also worked with Ezra to strengthen the religious activities of the Jews. The people started confessing their sins, making sacrifices and offerings, supporting the work of the Levites, and celebrating their festivals just as the Israelites did during the days of Moses. The people also pledged not to let their children marry anybody who was not a Jew.

Nehemiah returned to Susa, and when he returned to Jerusalem years later, he found the Jews had stopped practicing their religion properly. They worked and sold goods on the Sabbath. Levites had left to take jobs somewhere else because tithes were not given to support them and other Temple workers. Foreigners had offices in the Temple courtyard. All this made Nehemiah very angry – he threw out the furniture owned by the foreigners, closed Jerusalem's gates on the Sabbath, and reminded the people that those who ignored God's commands were punished by being captured.

The prophet **Malachi** reinforced his warnings because the Jews were not relying on God. These were their sins: offering imperfect animals in sacrifices, marrying non-Jews, being unfaithful in marriage, neglecting the tithe, not taking care of widows and orphans, and mistreating the poor and foreigners. Malachi also wrote about things to come in the future. Blessings and judgment would come, sometimes through a painful process. Through him, God said to the Jews:

> I won't change the way I deal with you: I will bless you if you honor me and obey my commands; I will punish you if you are arrogant and disobey. I will be compassionate if you return to me. I will send my messenger to prepare the way before me. Suddenly, the one you seek will come to the Temple. He will be like a refiner's fire or a soap and will purify the Levites. Then the Lord will have people who will bring offerings in righteousness, and their offerings will be acceptable to the Lord as they were previously.

The story continues in Chapter 8.

7
UNIQUE BOOKS IN THE OLD TESTAMENT

Several books of the Bible do not discuss historical events. The books of **Proverbs** and **Ecclesiastes** are about wisdom. **Jōb** is a story about why a person who has faith in God and leads a good life still experiences pain and suffering. **Jonah** is a short story of a man called by God to speak truth to a dangerous enemy. When he fails to do so, he suffers unusual consequences. The **Song of Solomon** is a dialogue between a young woman and her lover. **Psalms** is a collection of poems that reflect strong emotions and thoughts about events that took place among the Israelites.

Proverbs

Most of Proverbs was written by King Solomon. A proverb is a statement of a general truth and often deals with the right and wrong way to do things. In general, the proverbs say that those who follow these truths will avoid evil and be rewarded; those who don't follow their advice will suffer negative consequences.

Positive and negative statements are often coupled to provide a contrast between good and evil. Sometimes these are just one sentence long. For example, the last verse of chapter 3 states, "The wise inherit honor but fools inherit dishonor." In other cases, there are clusters of proverbs that discuss the same idea. Many of the sayings and short stories deal with money, justice, and sexual morality (many verses talk about avoiding the temptations of sex-related sins and making money the wrong way). The book has many reminders to its readers that they must constantly pursue wisdom and avoid doing evil things.

Ecclesiastes

This book contains the reflections of a wise king, probably King Solomon later in his reign. In contrast to Proverbs, wisdom is viewed more realistically – there is neither blind optimism for doing right nor skeptical pessimism for doing wrong. Instead, life is seen with its complexities and frustrations. Like life itself, the structure and content of the book's 12 chapters are disjointed, rambling in different directions and often repetitious.

The book begins with a Teacher exclaiming, "Everything is meaningless!" The endless cycles of life and nature never seem to change anything on earth. Gaining wisdom and knowledge brings sorrow and grief. Both have their limitations, and creating change to improve life is like "chasing after the wind – nothing is gained under the sun."

The Teacher tried to find happiness in different ways. He first pursued earthly pleasures – drinking, having sex, working hard, acquiring materials and wealth, and obtaining power. But when he reflected on his actions, none of them made him happy. Next, he thought about the pursuit of wisdom and the consequences of sinfulness, but he realized that both the wise and fools die the same death. Possessions acquired during life are passed on when a person dies to others who may be either wise or foolish, so the fruits of a life's labors may be squandered. Why pursue what you cannot keep?

The Teacher concluded that the best people can do to find true happiness is to honor God, enjoy their food and drinks, do good, and find meaningful work. He also concluded that instead of following fixed rules in every situation, the right behavior depends on the circumstances of each context – there is a right time for every human experience. The Teacher says good can come from negative experiences, but he still prefers the attributes of wisdom, even though life can be unfair. He concludes by encouraging people to enjoy life to the fullest, work hard, and embrace unexpected events as opportunities given by God to learn and grow.

Jōb

This long story includes many conversations about faith, obedience, rewards, punishments, good and evil, and why bad things happen to faithful people. God's loving and fair nature is questioned through a dialogue among the main characters: God and Satan, Job and his friends, and God and Job. The book is a story, not part of history (there is no clear author, date, or location), but its lessons are true.

The book begins by describing Job as a wealthy man living with his large family and 11,000 animals. He is "the greatest man in the east and is blameless, upright, faithful to God, and always careful to avoid doing evil." He makes sacrifices to God just in case members of his family have sinned.

Satan tells God that Job is only good and faithful because God blessed him in every way. Satan challenges God to take away all of Job's blessings to see if Job will still love God, saying that Job will curse God when the blessings are removed. God agrees to let Satan torment Job but forbids Satan from killing him.

Job and his family soon start suffering disasters. An enemy steals his animals and kills his servants. Fire kills his sheep and those caring for the flocks. Another enemy steals all his camels and kills all the servants except the messenger. Finally, a strong wind causes the house where his children were eating to collapse, killing everybody.

After hearing all this bad news, Job tears off his clothes and worships God by saying, "I came naked from my mother's womb, and I will leave the world with nothing. The Lord gives and the Lord takes away. Blessed be the name of the Lord." Job did not sin or blame God for these events.

God reminds Satan that Job stayed faithful even when he lost everything. Satan makes a new accusation, saying that Job will curse God if his own body suffers. God agrees to let Satan bring pain and sickness to Job, and his body develops painful sores from his head to his toes. Job's wife asks him, "Why do you still live the right way? Curse God and die!" Job replies, "Should we just accept good from God and not trouble?" and he does not sin or curse God.

When Job's friends hear what happened, they visit him to comfort him. They barely recognize him and weep with him silently for a week. Then they tell Job that his afflictions are due to sins Job committed and urge him to repent and obey to gain God's favor again. The friends say that God does not punish good people for nothing.

Job disagrees and says he has done nothing wrong. The friends mock Job's attitude and claims of innocence, but Job insists he has done nothing to deserve any of the afflictions. He gets irritated with their false accusations of his sinfulness and their self-righteous confidence in their simple answers to address his situation. He tells them to shut up! He is a broken man and suffers as he listens to his false accusers.

But Job is confused about how his life changed so quickly without committing any sin. He wonders how people can please a God who can be both just and forgiving to those who deserve punishment. God's ways are beyond human understanding. Job is sad about his life but believes God will eventually say he is innocent. His experience proves that suffering is not automatically linked to sinfulness and evil. And even if he dies, he says he will live again. "I know my redeemer lives and that in the end, God will still be standing. After my body is destroyed, I will still see God." Job does not know why certain things happen – sometimes the wicked prosper and life can be unfair. But his faith brings him hope that God's love and judgment will result in a "not guilty" verdict for him in the next life.

God has been listening to all their conversations and then speaks to Job. God asks him many questions that expose his ignorance about how the world works and

God's power. Job is overwhelmed and cannot answer God's questions.

God then turns to Job's friends in anger for incorrectly saying that suffering only occurs due to sin and that justice only occurs during one's lifetime. Easy answers may ease the conscience of the messenger, but they don't apply to complex situations.

The story ends very quickly without giving important details. God honors Job's humility and faithfulness and blesses him again with more than he originally had. But the story does not include anything about the deal between God and Satan. In the end, good prevails against evil because Job does not waver. Defeated again, Satan does not appear to God with another wager. Also, the story never explains why faithful followers suffer or why the wicked prosper, so readers are left to think about the answers for themselves. Life is unpredictable when good and evil forces coexist.

Jonah

In this brief story, God calls the prophet Jonah to speak truth and judgment to the people of Nineveh, the capital of the Assyrian empire. The story has few details but has many universal lessons that relate to human disobedience and the consequences of not following God's call, how nature can be used to show God's power, hatred toward foreigners, God's forgiveness for all people, and how we are disappointed when God shows love to those who we think don't deserve it.

Jonah was told to preach judgment to Nineveh, but instead of risking death, he takes a boat to Spain (2,000 miles in the other direction). A strong storm threatens to sink the ship, and the crew call to their gods to save the ship. The storm is so unusual that the crew knows somebody on the ship is cursed. They discover it is Jonah, and he explains that he is an Israelite who is disobeying God. He says the storm will stop if they throw him overboard. When the crew does this, the storm immediately stops, which makes everybody on board worship the Israelite God.

Jonah gets caught in seaweed and is swallowed by a large whale. Over a 3-day period, he struggles to stay alive inside the whale. After he promises God that he will go to Nineveh if he survives, the whale gets sick and vomits Jonah onto land.

Eventually Jonah goes to Nineveh and tells the people that the city will be destroyed because of their evil ways. The people believe his message and repent. The king orders everybody in the city to pray and stop their wickedness.

When seeing how the people of Nineveh respond, God shows compassion and does not destroy the city. This makes Jonah very angry – he wants the enemy to suffer. He tells God, "I know You are gracious and compassionate, slow to anger and generous in Your love, a God who does not like sending calamity."

Jonah goes up a hill near the city to watch what will happen. A worm eats the plant he used for shade and he gets very sunburned. Feeling sorry for himself, he says, "I'm so angry I'd rather be dead than alive." God tells Jonah, "You are worried about not having shade? Shouldn't I be concerned about a city with more than 120,000 children who are innocent and ignorant?" Jonah lacks love and forgiveness, even though the God he follows is loving and forgiving.

Song of Solomon

The unknown author of this short story uses a dialogue written in poetry to describe a perfect love story between a young woman and her boyfriend. The romance has no conflict, and the author uses vivid images of plants and animals to describe the couple's attraction to each other. The story affirms that physical love is a blessing within a marriage.

The story describes the couple – the young maiden is tan from working in a vineyard and the man is well-respected. He falls in love with her at first sight and thinks about his wedding day with her. They long to be with each other and think about the features of the other's beautiful body and movements. Although there are many eligible women around him, she is unique in having both external and internal beauty – this humble and sincere worker is the only one for him. She dreams about him and is sad when she wakes up and finds that he is not there. When they get married and leave town together, they show their love for one another.

Psalms

Poetry was used in some books of the Bible, and some books were written totally in poetry form. The book of Psalms has 150 poems written by David and other authors that reflect strong emotions and thoughts related to what took place among the Israelites. Most relate in some way to the concepts of good and evil. About half of the psalms deal with prayers during times of trouble, and some simply praise God. Rather than using words that rhyme, the psalms often contain repeating ideas. The authors usually used male pronouns and nouns (he, his, him, man) to describe God and all people. The first psalm appears below.

Psalm 1 *(The Righteous and Wicked Contrasted)*
Blessed is the man who does not walk in the counsel of
    the wicked,
Nor stands in the path with sinners, nor sits in seats with
    scoffers!
But his delight is in the law of the Lord,
And he meditates on His laws day and night.
He will be like a tree firmly planted by streams of water,
Which yields its fruit in its season
And whose leaf does not wither.
Whatever he does prospers.
Not so with the wicked! They are like chaff the wind
    blows away.
Therefore the wicked will not stand in the judgment,
Nor will sinners assemble with the righteous.
For the Lord knows the way of the righteous,
But the way of the wicked will perish.

PART 2

THE
NEW TESTAMENT

8
THE MESSIAH ARRIVES

Background

Malachi's prophecies were written in 420 BC and are the last record of the Old Testament prophets. Many Jews lived outside of Palestine, mainly in Babylonia and Egypt, and their communities were quite large. To maintain their faith, these communities set up places of worship (synagogues) that were led by a religious scholar (rabbi) who read and explained the scriptures to the Israelites.

During the 400 years following Malachi's prophecies, many important events took place that influenced the Jews.

- The Greeks, led by Alexander the Great, conquered Palestine and many parts of the world. The Greeks brought new religious and political ideas about the world, and the Greek language became widely spoken and written (Hebrew and Aramaic were also used by the Jews). Jewish communities enjoyed peace during Alexander's reign.

- After Alexander died, Judaism was banned. A few Jews rebelled because they were required to make sacrifices to other gods. A revolt spread throughout Palestine, and the Greeks were eventually expelled in 142 BC. (Hanukkah celebrates this victory.)

- The Romans conquered Palestine in 63 BC and controlled Jerusalem. They did not tolerate rebellion and executed many Jewish leaders. In 37 BC Herod the Great became the king and started constructing many buildings, including a larger Temple in Jerusalem. When he died in 4 BC, Rome put other leaders in his place.

The People of Palestine

During this 400-year period, Greek ways of thinking became attractive to many Jews, and differences emerged among the Jews about how they should live in a world while preserving their faith.

- The *Pharisees* were a small but influential group who focused on strict obedience to God's commands. They wanted to be separate from the world, did not relate to nonbelievers, and stayed away from foreign influences. They stressed being very religious and held rigid views of right and wrong. They followed more rules to ensure they did not come close to breaking any of God's commands. They were very proud and showed their religion to others in very obvious ways.
- The *Sadducees* were another small but influential group, but they focused on morality and did not believe in supernatural powers. They accepted foreign ideas, especially those of the Greeks. They were wealthy and well-educated and did not follow the additional rules the Pharisees followed.
- The *Essenes* withdrew from the world. This small group retreated to remote areas, mainly into the desert.
- *Zealots* wanted to use physical force to ensure no foreign power controlled their lives. They were willing to die for their cause.

Other types of people lived in Palestine. Some were labeled based on where they lived, such as the impure Samaritans and Galileans who were hated because they had often intermarried with non-Jews or were not Jewish at all. (Galilee was the northern part of Palestine, Samaria was the central part, and Judea was the southern part that was previously known as Judah.) Galileans were also known for being rebellious against foreign authority. Some groups were distinct based on their profession, such as the scribes, who wrote important documents (often religious in nature), and members of the Sanhedrin, a diverse group of leaders who watched over the religious life of the Jews and could punish

Jews. Some were known for their allegiance: Herodians followed Roman traditions and beliefs, and Hellenists followed Greek traditions and beliefs.

Because of the immigration of non-Jews into Palestine and the emigration of Jews out of Palestine, most of the people living in Palestine 2,000 years ago were not Jews, and more than 80% of the Jews lived elsewhere. Palestine did not have a good system of roads, and it was not easy to travel in the area. People usually walked or used a donkey or mule. A few basic inns existed along the roads, so many travelers stayed with their friends and family when they traveled.

Many prophets had written about a Servant-King who would come and bring the nation back to glory. The Jews wondered when God would send this leader and why it was taking so long. Events in the region made the Jews think that somebody would deliver them from oppression. Roman brutality reminded them of when their ancestors were mistreated in Egypt and conquered by other nations. It had been 400 years since they last heard from a prophet about somebody who would suddenly appear. They watched closely for the coming Messiah (*Christ* in Greek), the Anointed One who would come and save them as Rome crushed Jewish rebel leaders and executed them slowly by nailing them alive to crosses throughout the region.

This chapter and chapters 9–11 describe the important events that took place in the life of Jesus and his main teachings as they were recorded by four men. Two authors were eyewitnesses who followed Jesus closely and were among the first disciples (John was a fisherman and Matthew was a tax collector). The other two authors were Mark, a close friend of Peter, and Luke, a Gentile doctor who traveled with Paul and investigated the stories told about Jesus. Mark's account was the first one written, and John's account was written last and includes stories and details that the others did not include. The authors had a different audience and their own style and perspectives, so the accounts are somewhat different. Collectively, they are known as the "gospels" (good news about Jesus).

Two Babies Are Born

In 5 BC when Herod was the Roman king in charge of Judah, a priest named Zechariah and his wife Elizabeth had grown old without having any children. Zechariah was told by an angel that his wife would have a son and his name should be John. He was not to drink wine, and the Holy Spirit would fill him. He would bring many disobedient Jews to God and prepare the people for the Lord.

When Elizabeth was six months pregnant, the same angel appeared to a young teenager named Mary who lived in Nazareth, a town in Galilee. She was engaged to Joseph, a descendant of King David. The angel greeted Mary, who was confused and afraid when she heard from a complete stranger who suddenly appeared. The angel said, "Don't be afraid. You will give birth to a son and are to call him Jesus. He will be great – God will give him the throne of King David, his ancestor. He will reign over Jacob's descendants forever."

Mary wondered how it could happen – she was still a virgin and not yet married. The angel said that God's spirit was the father and that her relative Elizabeth was pregnant. Mary was amazed that Elizabeth could be pregnant and went to see her. When Mary arrived, God revealed to Elizabeth what had happened to Mary. When Elizabeth had her baby three months later, Zechariah told everybody that John would be a prophet that spoke about the coming Messiah.

Jesus Is Born

When Mary returned home, her fiancé Joseph found out she was pregnant. He was a good man and thought of divorcing her quietly (they were legally bound to be married). But an angel told him in a dream that God's Spirit was the father. Mary's son was to be named Jesus, for he would save people from their sins. This had been predicted by the prophet Isaiah: "The virgin will conceive and bear a son, and he will be called Immanuel" (meaning "God with us"). So Joseph went back to Nazareth and married Mary.

Just before Mary was to give birth, the Roman emperor Caesar Augustus ordered everybody to go to their hometown where they would be counted for a census. Mary and Joseph traveled south from Nazareth to Bethlehem, a town close to Jerusalem. The town was full of people returning to be counted, and there was no place for Mary and Joseph to stay. They found space in a barn, which is where Mary gave birth to Jesus. Mary used a manger (a feeding trough for animals) as a crib.

That night, an angel appeared to shepherds who were watching their flocks nearby. They were very frightened, but the angel told them, "Don't be afraid. I have good news that will make everyone happy! A Savior was born today in Bethlehem – he is the Messiah, the Lord. Go see him, he is the one wrapped up and lying in a manger." Then many other angels appeared and shouted, "Glory to God in the highest heaven and on earth. He will bring peace."

The shepherds hurried into town and found the family and the baby. After seeing him, they told others what had happened, and everybody was amazed by their story.

Foreign Priests Visit Jesus

Before Jesus was born, priests from Persia (Magi) who studied the stars saw a bright light in the sky that convinced them that a new king was born in Judah. They traveled hundreds of miles and went to Jerusalem to ask King Herod where the Jews' king was born. The thought of another king worried Herod and other leaders in Jerusalem. Herod found out that the Jewish Messiah was to be born in Bethlehem, and he told the Magi to find the boy and come back to tell him where he was. (Herod said he wanted to worship the boy himself.)

The bright star hovered over Bethlehem a few miles away, and the Magi found Jesus with his parents. They worshipped Jesus and gave him gifts of gold, frankincense, and myrrh. Before they left, they were warned in a dream to use a different route to return home and not tell Herod where Jesus was staying.

After the Magi left, Joseph had a dream that he should take Mary and Jesus to Egypt because Herod was looking for Jesus to kill him. Joseph woke up and immediately left in the middle of the night for Egypt. When Herod realized the Magi had left without telling him where Jesus was, he was furious and gave orders to kill all the boys in Bethlehem and its vicinity who were two years old or younger. (Jeremiah predicted this would happen.)

The family stayed in Egypt until Herod died. This fulfilled what the prophet Hosea said: "I called my son out of Egypt." Joseph and Mary returned with Jesus to their home in Nazareth, whose ancestors went back many generations and included Abraham, Isaac, Jacob, Judah, Boaz, Jesse, David, Solomon, Rehoboam, Hezekiah, Amos, and Josiah. Two foreign women, Rahab and Ruth, were among his ancestors.

The Family Visits Jerusalem

Every year the family went to Jerusalem for the Passover festival. When Jesus was 12 years old, Mary and Joseph accidentally left him behind when they returned to Nazareth after the festival. After traveling with their friends and relatives, they realized Jesus was missing, and they returned to Jerusalem to look for him. They eventually found him in the Temple as he sat among the teachers, listening to them and asking questions. Everyone who heard him was amazed at his understanding, insights, and answers, even though he was still a young boy. Mary scolded him for making his parents worry, but Jesus said, "Why did you spend so much time looking for me? Didn't you know I had to be in my Father's house?" Then they all returned to Nazareth. Jesus was an obedient child and grew in wisdom and pleased God and everybody who knew him. When he grew up, he became a carpenter.

John Emerges from the Wilderness

John lived in the wilderness as an adult and came out of the desert when he was 30 years old. He wore strange clothes and ate strange food. He traveled near the Jordan River and told people to change their ways and ask for their sins to be forgiven. He told people, "Repent, for the kingdom of heaven is coming." His arrival was predicted by the prophet Isaiah, who wrote: "A voice calls in the wilderness, 'Prepare the way for the Lord, make his paths straight and the rough places smooth. Everybody will see God's saving work.'"[2]

Thousands of people heard John and confessed their sins. John baptized people in the river and was known as John the Baptist. When he saw Pharisees and Sadducees coming to see what was happening, he spoke to them harshly.

> You poisonous snakes! Produce fruit that shows you have repented. Don't think you can say to yourselves, "We have Abraham as our father." God can raise children of Abraham from these stones. Every tree that doesn't produce good fruit will be cut down and burned.

Scribes and Levites from Jerusalem came and asked him if he was the Messiah. John said no, but he quoted Isaiah and said he was "the voice crying in the wilderness, 'Make straight the way for the Lord.'" He was saying that the Messiah was coming soon.

When people asked him what they should do next, John said, "Anyone who has two shirts should share one with a person who has none. Anyone who has food should share in the same way." When the despised tax collectors who worked for the Romans came to be baptized and asked what they should do, John told them not to collect any more than they were required to collect. When soldiers asked him what they should do, he said, "Don't force people to pay you or accuse people falsely – be content with what you are paid."

People wondered if John was the Messiah, but he said, "I baptize you with water, but another will come soon who

---

[2] Whenever a king traveled at that time, he would send workers ahead to ensure the route was direct and smooth, thus making the king's trip faster and more comfortable.

is more powerful than I am. He will baptize you with the Holy Spirit. He will gather the wheat into his barn, but he will burn up all the chaff."

Jesus went to the Jordan River to be baptized by John. They were relatives who were born at about the same time and were friends. When John saw Jesus coming, he said, "Look, it's the Lamb of God who takes away the sins of the world!" He didn't think it was right for him to baptize Jesus, but Jesus said, "This needs to happen so I fulfill all the signs of righteousness."

So John baptized Jesus, and when Jesus came out of the water, the sky opened and God's Spirit came down in the form of a dove and landed on him. A voice from the sky said, "This is my Son who I love. He pleases me." Those who were there also heard the voice.

Jesus Is Tested and Starts to Preach

Many people fasted and prayed after being baptized, and Jesus was no different. He was full of the Holy Spirit and went into the wilderness. After eating nothing for 40 days, he was very hungry, weak, and vulnerable. Satan came as an evil spirit and tempted him by saying, "If you really are the Son of God, tell this stone to become bread." Jesus said, "It is written: 'We are not to live on bread alone, but on the words of God.'"

Satan led Jesus to the top of the Temple and said, "If you are the Son of God, throw yourself down. For it is written: 'God will command your angels to guard you carefully. They will lift you up.'" But Jesus said, "It is also written, 'Do not put the Lord your God to a test.'"

Satan then led Jesus to a high place and showed him all the kingdoms of the world, saying, "I will give you power to control all of this. It's all mine, and I can give it to anybody. If you worship me, it will all be yours." Jesus said, "I order you to leave, for it is written: 'Worship and serve only the Lord your God.'" After these three temptations failed, Satan withdrew and waited for another chance to tempt or trap Jesus, who continued praying and fasting in the wilderness.

John was arrested when he criticized Herod's son because of all the evil things he had done. When Jesus found out what happened to John, he started preaching John's message, "Repent, for the kingdom of heaven is about to come." Preaching in that area was another prediction Isaiah made about the coming of the Messiah.

Jesus then went to Nazareth where he had been raised as a child and worked as an adult. One Sabbath day, he went to the synagogue as he usually did. Everybody knew him, and he stood up in front of the congregation and read what Isaiah wrote: "The Spirit of the Lord is on me, because God has anointed me to proclaim good news to the poor. God has sent me to proclaim freedom for the prisoners and recovery of sight for the blind, to set the oppressed free and proclaim the Year of Jubilee." This well-recognized part of Isaiah's writings was about the Messiah. Then he said, "Today this scripture is fulfilled."

Everybody was saying nice things about him and all were amazed at his wise words. They wondered if he was the same Jesus they knew who was a carpenter and the son of Joseph and Mary. But their happiness quickly changed to anger when Jesus scolded them and other Jews.

> No prophet is welcomed in his hometown. Elijah didn't help any of the Israelites but instead helped a widow in another country. There were many in Israel with leprosy when Elisha was the prophet, but only Naaman, the Syrian, was cleansed.

Everybody in the synagogue was furious. He implied that he was the Messiah but showed a preference for foreigners! Jesus walked out and went to the top of the town's highest hill, a place where people were taken to be stoned. The people followed him, but when he got to the top of the hill, he turned around and walked down the hill through the crowd. Nobody touched him and he never performed any miracles in Nazareth.

Jesus then went to Capernaum and spoke in the synagogue, and everybody was amazed by how he understood the scriptures. A man in the audience who was possessed by a demon yelled in a loud voice, "Go away! What do you want from us? Have you come to destroy us? I know you are the Holy One of God!"

Jesus firmly said to him, "Be quiet and come out of him!" The demon threw the man to the ground and came out. Everybody was amazed that Jesus had authority and power over evil spirits – the demons he confronted came out of people! News about Jesus and his powers spread quickly throughout the region.

Jesus Calls His First Followers

Jesus attracted large crowds who wanted to hear his views and see his amazing powers. When he first preached on the shore of the Sea of Galilee, the crowd got so large that he was pressed against the water. He saw two empty boats on the shoreline and pushed one of them into the water. He got in the boat and spoke to the crowd from it.

The boat belonged to brothers named Simon and Andrew. When Jesus finished talking, he got out of the boat and told them to take it into deep waters and put down their nets. Simon said, "We worked all night and caught nothing. But we will do it." When they did, they caught so many fish that their nets started to rip. They called their two partners on shore (brothers named James and John) and had them bring their boat to help haul in all the fish. These fishermen caught so many fish that both boats started to sink.

Everybody was amazed at the size of the catch. They wondered how a carpenter knew so much about fishing and also understood the scriptures so well. When Simon came on shore with all the fish, he fell at the feet of Jesus and said, "Depart from me, Lord. I'm a sinful man." Jesus told Simon not to be afraid and gave him the name Peter (meaning "rock") and told him he would soon be catching men, not fish. In fact, Jesus told Peter that he would be the rock on which a new kingdom would be created, and the powers of death would not overcome it. All four men left their boats and nets in the hands of their parents and followed Jesus.

The next day, Jesus told Philip, a friend of Peter and Andrew, to follow him. Philip told his friend Bartholomew about Jesus, who wondered if anything good could come out of Nazareth. Philip said, "Come and see!"

Jesus then had six men who followed him closely. Such people were known as "disciples" – they dedicated themselves to learning from a wise teacher, the way an apprentice is guided by a master. (It was common for wise teachers to have people follow and learn from them.)

Jesus went to the home of Simon Peter whose mother-in-law had a high fever. Peter asked Jesus to help her. After Jesus commanded the fever to leave her, she got up at once and began serving them. Word spread that Jesus could heal the sick, and that evening, people started bringing him those who were sick in some way. He laid his hands on each one and healed them.

The next morning, Jesus went out to be alone. People found him and tried to keep him from leaving, but Jesus said he had come to preach good news of the kingdom of God in many areas.

9
THE ACTS OF JESUS

Jesus kept preaching in synagogues and performing miracles. He had unusual charisma and acted with authority. News about him quickly spread, and people brought him those who were ill or had physical ailments. Large crowds of people from all over Palestine and large cities east of the Jordan (most of them were Gentiles) started following him. He often associated with non-Jews and people considered by religious Jews to be immoral. Many of his actions helped non-Jews and those living on the margins of society (women, those with a disability, those possessed by an evil spirit).

Jesus performed many miracles. Sometimes he did it to make a point, and sometimes it was simply an act of kindness. He healed people's bodies, emotions, and spirits. He intentionally performed miracles on the Sabbath in order to teach about God's priorities – the Pharisees believed these miracles were a type of work, which was prohibited on the day of rest. This chapter describes the important acts and teachings of Jesus after he became a public figure in Galilee when he was 30 years old.

Unusual Encounters and Miracles

A Wedding Miracle

Soon after Jesus spoke from the boat in the Sea of Galilee, he went to a wedding in Cana with his mother. On the third day of the celebration, his mother told him that there was no more wine. Jesus said he wasn't ready to reveal his powers, but Mary told the servants to do whatever he said. Six large stone water jars stood nearby that Jews used to wash their hands before a meal. Each held at least 20 gallons of water. Jesus told the servants to fill the jars with water and then take it to the master of the banquet.

The master tasted it but did not know where it came from. Then he called the bridegroom aside and said, "Everyone serves the best wine first and then the cheaper wine after the guests have had too much to drink. But you have saved the best until now!" The water had turned into more than 100 gallons of fine wine after many people had already had too much to drink!

Samaritan Woman

Jesus traveled with his disciples through Samaria, a region avoided by Jews. He arrived at a well at noon and sat down while the disciples went to get food. When a Samaritan woman arrived, Jesus asked her for a drink. She said, "You're a Jew and I'm a Samaritan woman. Why do you ask me for a drink?"

Jesus told her that if she knew who he was, she would ask him for a drink and he would give her living water, a term referring to fresh water in a deep well. He said that those who drink from the water he gives will never be thirsty, and "it becomes a spring of water in your soul and brings eternal life." She didn't see how that was possible because he didn't have anything to get water. But she wanted this type of water so she did not have to visit the well in the heat in middle of the day.

Jesus told her to get her husband, but she said she didn't have one. Jesus replied, "You're right. That's because you have had five husbands, and the man you live with now is not your husband." The embarrassed woman quickly changed the subject and said he was a prophet and said her ancestors worshipped on this mountain, but the Jews said the Samaritans had to worship in Jerusalem. Jesus told her that a time was coming when people did not have to worship in any one place; rather, "True worshippers will worship God in the Spirit."

When the woman said she knew the Messiah was coming, Jesus said to her, "I am that man." She then went quickly into town and told everybody, "Come see a man who told me everything I ever did. Could this be the Messiah?" Many people came to see him, and many believed in him. Jesus stayed there for two days, and even more Samaritans started following Jesus and believed he was the Messiah. In contrast, when he spoke to the Jews, he was vague about who he was and referred to himself indirectly as the Son of Man.

A Secret Meeting in the Night

A Jewish leader named Nicodemus visited Jesus secretly during the night and was curious to learn more about him. Jesus told him, "Nobody can see the kingdom of God unless they are born again." Nicodemus was puzzled and asked, "How can anybody be born when they are already old? They can't be born a second time!" Jesus responded and described a new covenant.

> Nobody can enter the kingdom of God unless they are born of water and the Spirit. The Spirit gives birth to one's spirit. The Son of Man must be lifted up so everyone who believes may have eternal life. For God loved the world so much that God's Son was sent into the world so that whoever believes in him will not die but will live forever. The Son existed before the creation of the world, and God didn't send him into the world to condemn the world. He has come to save the world. Those who believe and follow him are not condemned; those who don't will stand condemned. Light has come into the world, but people love darkness because their deeds are evil. Those who live by the truth come into the light so what they do can be seen.

Zacchaeus the Tax Collector

A short wealthy man named Zacchaeus was the chief tax collector in Jericho and was in a crowd when Jesus came to the city. He climbed a tree so he could see Jesus walk by. When Jesus reached the tree, he saw Zacchaeus and told him to come down so they could eat together. Everybody knew who Zacchaeus was, and they started gossiping that Jesus was going to be a guest of a sinner. But Zacchaeus was a changed man and told Jesus, "Lord, I will now give half of my possessions to the poor, and if I have cheated anybody out of anything, I will pay back four times the amount."

Jesus told him, "Today you and those in your house have been saved. This man is a son of Abraham. The Son of Man came to save the lost."

A Rich Young Ruler

A young leader asked Jesus what must be done to inherit eternal life. Jesus said the man must obey the 10 commands. The man said he had obeyed all of them since he was a boy. Jesus then told him, "You still lack one thing. Sell everything you have and give to the poor, and you will have treasure in heaven. Then follow me."

When the man heard this, he was very sad because he was very rich. Jesus looked at him and said to those who were there, "It's very hard for the rich to enter the kingdom of God! It's easier for a camel to go through the eye of a needle than for someone who is rich to enter the kingdom of God." Those who heard this asked Jesus who could be saved. Jesus replied, "What is impossible for people is possible with God."[3]

---

[3] The "eye of a needle" was a very small opening in Jerusalem's wall. A camel would need to be completely unloaded and lying flat on a board, then dragged through on a wooden plank in order to get through the gate. The message implies that a person cannot inherit eternal life simply by becoming very humble and

Jesus Heals Many Types of People

Jesus was teaching in a house that was very crowded with people from all over Palestine; Pharisees and scribes sat in the front row. Jesus had been healing many people, and some men came to the house carrying a paralyzed man on a mat. When they couldn't get in the door, they went on the roof, took off the tiles, and slowly lowered the man on his mat with ropes, down to where Jesus was talking. Everybody watched the man descend from the roof. When Jesus saw their faith, he told the man on the mat that his sins were forgiven.

The Pharisees and scribes wondered what kind of man would speak such blasphemy, for only God can forgive sins. Jesus knew what they were thinking and asked, "Which is easier, to say, 'Your sins are forgiven,' or to say, 'Get up and walk'? But I want you to know that the Son of Man has authority to forgive sins." Jesus told the paralyzed man, "Get up and take your mat home." Immediately the man stood up and took what he had been lying on and went home.

On another occasion, a Roman centurion asked Jesus for help. His servant was paralyzed at home and in great pain. When Jesus offered to go to his home to help, the soldier said, "Lord, I don't deserve to have you in my house. Just say the word, and my servant will be healed. I understand authority – I have soldiers under me, and if I tell one of them, 'Go,' he goes." Jesus was amazed by the centurion's faith and told him, "Truly, I haven't found anyone in Israel with such faith! Go, it has been done, just as you believed it would." The servant at his home was healed at that moment.

When Jesus was in Jerusalem for a Jewish festival, he went to a pool that had healing powers. Many people with disabilities would rest near the pool, and one man had been there for 38 years. When Jesus saw him and learned how long he had been there, he asked the man if he wanted to

---

poor — God's help is needed. In addition, a person's possessions may be a stumbling block to living an obedient life.

get well. The man told Jesus that he didn't have anybody to help him into the pool when the water stirred. Someone else always got to the water first and got healed. Jesus told him, "Get up! Pick up your mat and walk." The man was instantly cured. He picked up his mat and walked out of the pool area.

Since this took place on the Sabbath, Jewish leaders reminded the man that it was forbidden to carry a mat on the Sabbath. But he told them that the man who made him well told him to pick up his mat and walk. They asked him who told him to do this, but the man had no idea. When Jesus found him at the Temple later, the healed man told the Jewish leaders that it was Jesus who healed him.

Jesus Heals Those with Evil Spirits

Among those Jesus encountered were people who had evil spirits living in them. When he met them, they recognized him as the Son of God because evil spirits know who he is. But when the spirits revealed what they knew about him, Jesus would stop them and not let them speak because he didn't want people to know he was the Messiah until the right time.

When Jesus needed time away from the crowds, he went to the coast of Phoenicia with only his disciples. A Greek woman living there begged Jesus to have mercy on her daughter who was demon-possessed. Jesus ignored her and told his disciples, "I was sent only to the lost sheep of Israel." But she kept bothering them and became a nuisance. She knelt before Jesus and asked for help. Jesus told her, "It's not right to take the children's bread and toss it to the dogs."

She responded in an unusual way: "But Lord, even the dogs eat the crumbs that fall from their master's table." Jesus said to her, "Woman, you have great faith! The demon is gone." She went home and found her child lying on the bed without the demon.

Later, Jesus took an unusual trip to a Gentile region east of the Sea of Galilee to help two men who had many demons. They lived in tombs, cut their bodies with sharp objects, didn't wear any clothes, and were so violent that nobody could be close to them. When Jesus approached them, they shouted, "Why have you come to use your power on us?"

Jesus asked them what they were called. They said "Legion" because there were so many demons in the men. (The term *legion* refers to a group of several thousand Roman soldiers.) The demons saw a large herd of pigs in the distance and asked Jesus to cast them into the pigs. Jesus pointed at the pigs and said "Go" to the demons. The demons left the men, entered the pigs, and the entire herd ran down a hill and off a cliff into the sea.

Those tending the pigs told everybody in the region what happened. Many people went to see Jesus and the men who had the demons, who were sitting at Jesus's feet, dressed in normal clothes, and in their right minds. But the people asked Jesus to leave – they were afraid of him, and he had just killed their pigs, a very valuable source of income. One of the men wanted to go with him to Galilee, but Jesus told him to go home and tell everybody what God had done for him.

The Dead Come to Life

One of Jesus's best friends was a man named Lazarus. His sister was Mary Magdalene who had been delivered from demons. Lazarus was very sick, and Mary and her sister Martha sent word to Jesus to come as fast as he could to heal his good friend.

But Jesus stayed where he was for two more days, then he told his disciples it was time to go see Lazarus because he was dead. It took them two more days to get there, and when they arrived, Lazarus had been in a tomb for four days.

Many Jews were there to comfort Martha and Mary. When Martha heard Jesus was close, she ran to him and said, "Lord, if you had been here, my brother would not have died." Jesus told her that Lazarus would rise from the dead. Martha said she knew he would eventually rise in the last resurrection, but Jesus said, "I am the resurrection and the life – those who believe in me will always live, even though they die. Do you believe this?" She replied, "Yes, Lord, I believe you are the Messiah, the Son of God, who has come into the world."

When he went to the tomb, Mary was there along with many Jews who came to comfort the sisters. Mary also complained that that if he had come sooner, Lazarus would not be dead. When Jesus saw her and all the Jews crying, he knelt and wept as he was overcome with emotion. Lazarus was young but was now buried in a cave, and a large stone blocked the entrance.

Then Jesus told others to move the stone. Martha was aghast and said, "Lord! He won't smell good!" (Martha was constantly trying to do things right in order to make a good impression.) Jesus told her it was to show people the power of belief in God. After the stone was removed, Jesus looked up and said, "Father, thank you for hearing me. I know you always hear me, but I say this so the people here will believe that you sent me."

Jesus then said in a loud voice into the cave, "Lazarus, come out!" The dead man came out with his hands and feet wrapped with strips of linen. A cloth was around his face. Jesus told those who were there to take off his graveclothes and let him go. Lazarus was alive again!

Jesus Behaves in Unusual Ways

Jesus Associates with Sinners

Jesus saw a tax collector named Levi sitting at his tax booth. He told Levi to follow him. Levi got up, left everything behind, and followed Jesus. Later, Levi (also called Matthew) held a large banquet for Jesus at his house, and many tax collectors and others were there. But the Pharisees and scribes complained about Jesus's disciples and asked him why he ate and drank with tax collectors and sinners. Jesus answered, "Healthy people don't need a doctor, but the sick do. I have come to call sinners to repent, not the righteous."

The religious leaders continued questioning Jesus. They noted that the disciples of John and the Pharisees often fasted and prayed, but those who followed Jesus were happy with their eating and drinking. Jesus answered, "Can you make the friends of the bridegroom fast while he is with them? But the time will come when the bridegroom will be taken from them; in those days they will fast." Then Jesus told them this parable:

> No one tears a piece out of a new garment to patch an old one, and nobody pours new wine into old wineskins because the new wine will expand and burst the skins, ruining the wine and the wineskins. New wine must be poured into new wineskins, and nobody who drinks old wine wants the new, for they say, "The old is better."

(Jesus was saying that people are more comfortable with the usual ways of thinking and doing things and resist new things and ideas. Old wine skins are inflexible, and change is hard.)

Jesus Disrupts the Temple

When Jesus was in Jerusalem to celebrate the Passover, he went to the Temple courtyard. He saw people selling animals for sacrifices and sitting at tables changing money. He became very mad and made a whip and drove all the animals out of the courtyard. He also turned over the tables which scattered the money across the ground. He told the men, "Stop turning my Father's house into a market! It is written, 'My house shall be a house of prayer,' but you have made it a den of thieves!"

The Jews asked Jesus what sign he could give to prove his authority and justify his actions. Jesus said, "Destroy this Temple, and I will raise it in three days." They replied, "It took many years to build this Temple. You are going to raise it in three days?" The Temple Jesus was talking about was his own body.

Jesus and the Sea of Galilee

One evening, Jesus and his disciples were in a boat on the lake. A furious storm suddenly caused large waves to crash over the sides of the boat, and it began to sink. Jesus was sleeping as the boat was filling with water. The disciples woke him up because they thought they were all about to drown. Jesus told them, "Men of little faith, why are you afraid?" He got up and told the winds and waves to stop, and everything became totally calm. The men in the boat were amazed that even the winds and waves obeyed him!

The Twelve Disciples

While Jesus attracted huge crowds as he moved around Palestine, there were 12 men who were his closest disciples. Jesus called these dedicated disciples "apostles." They were:
- Peter (Simon) and his brother Andrew (fishermen and small business owners)
- James and John (fishing partners of Peter and Andrew)
- Philip (the fishermen's friend) and his friend Bartholomew (also known as Nathaniel)
- Matthew (a tax collector, also known as Levi)
- Thomas (also known as Didymus)
- James (son of Alphaeus)
- Simon the Zealot
- Judas (son of another man named James)
- Judas Iscariot (a man with financial expertise).

Jesus told the 12 disciples and many others to spread word in towns and villages that he was coming to visit. He gave them power and authority to drive out all demons, heal the sick, and announce the kingdom of God. They took nothing with them, and when they entered a house, they first said, "Peace be to this house." If someone there was promoting peace, they stayed there. But if people in the town didn't welcome them, they left the town and shook the dust off their feet as a sign against them. They went in pairs proclaiming the good news about Jesus and healed people everywhere.

Many women also followed Jesus, including Mary Magdalene, Joanna (the manager of Herod's household), and Susanna. These women supported Jesus and the disciples with their own money.

John the Baptist

John the Baptist was in prison as Jesus's ministry grew. John's followers told him what Jesus was doing and saying, and John sent men to ask Jesus, "Are you the one we are expecting to come, or should we expect someone else?"

Jesus told the messengers to tell John that "the blind receive sight, the paralyzed walk, those with leprosy are cleansed, the deaf hear, the dead are raised, and good news is proclaimed to the poor." These were signs that he was the Messiah. Then Jesus spoke about John to the religious leaders: "John is the one the prophets wrote about when they wrote: 'I will send my messenger ahead of you, who will prepare your way before you.'"

John was soon killed while in prison because he had told King Herod that he should not have married his brother's wife. The king's new wife ordered the execution, and the king reluctantly agreed.

10
THE TEACHINGS OF JESUS CHALLENGE RELIGIOUS TRADITIONS

Jesus was the most interesting person to speak to the Jews in centuries, but his messages and actions confused many people. He mainly taught by telling stories that people would understand. He could quote any scripture at any time, even though he hadn't been trained as a rabbi. He provided new ideas about the commands Moses had written, and he didn't follow strict religious rules.

The number of people who started following Jesus threatened the usual religious activities. Many who looked for the coming Messiah assumed the person would bring military victories and overthrow the Romans, but Jesus had a different message. He spoke about the kingdom of God and kingdom of heaven as if they were near, present, and coming.

Jesus had very different views about the scriptures from what the religious leaders believed. At times, his teaching directly conflicted with what had been written. He would say, "You have heard it said … but I say to you …." Sometimes his messages were hard to understand, and sometimes his messages related to things that would happen in the future. He only condemned those who were very religious and who used religion to benefit themselves. He focused on spiritual growth rather than changing the government – he never criticized the cruel Romans. Jesus said the problem was the inappropriate religious beliefs and expectations held by very religious Jews.

What Defiles a Person

Religious Jews did not eat until they washed their hands in a certain way, and they followed other traditions related to cleanliness. Some Pharisees and scribes saw Jesus and his disciples eating food without washing their hands and asked why they ate with dirty hands. Jesus said that food was clean.

> Isaiah was right when he called you hypocrites. You have let go of the commands of God and only follow human traditions. Eating with unclean hands does not make a person bad. It's what comes out of a person's heart that shows their sin. Evil comes from a person's heart, such as being unfaithful, being selfish and mean, plotting evil, jealousy, telling lies, and being proud. These evils come from inside a person.

Jesus had dinner with a Pharisee and didn't wash his hands first. Jesus told him, "You Pharisees clean the outside of the cup and dish, but inside you are full of greed and wickedness. A sign that you are clean inside is that you are generous to the poor."

The Sabbath

When Jesus and his disciples walked through fields of grain during the Sabbath, they picked some heads of grain and ate the kernels. Some Pharisees asked Jesus why he was doing what was unlawful on the Sabbath. Jesus answered them:

> Haven't you read what David did when he and his friends were hungry? They entered the house of God and ate the blessed bread that was lawful only for priests to eat. People were not made for the Sabbath; the Sabbath was made for people. God said, "I desire mercy, not sacrifice," so you shouldn't condemn the innocent. If your sheep falls in a pit on the Sabbath, won't you lift it out?

When Jesus was teaching in the synagogue on the Sabbath, a man with a shriveled hand was there. The Pharisees and scribes watched closely to see if he would heal somebody on the Sabbath. Jesus told the man to stand up in front of everyone and asked the religious leaders, "Which is lawful on the Sabbath: to do good or evil, to save life or destroy it?" When nobody responded, Jesus told the man to stretch out his hand. When he did, his hand was completely healed. The Pharisees and scribes were furious with Jesus for "working" on the Sabbath.

The Good Samaritan

A religious leader who wanted to test Jesus asked him what must be done for a person to live forever. Jesus responded that people should do what was written in the Law. The leader quoted the Law: "Love the Lord your God with all your heart, with all your soul, with all your strength, and with all your mind" and "Love your neighbor as yourself." Jesus replied, "You are correct. Do this and you will live."

But the clever leader asked Jesus, "Who is my neighbor?" Jesus replied with a story.

> A man walked down the dangerous road from Jerusalem to Jericho and was attacked by robbers. They stripped him, beat him, and left him half dead. A priest walking by moved to the other side of the road when he saw the man. A Levite also saw the man and also passed him on the other side of the road. But a Samaritan came along and saw the half-dead man and felt sorry for him. He cleaned and covered his wounds, then put the man on his donkey and took him to the nearest inn. He told the innkeeper to take care of him and he gave two days' wages to the innkeeper and said, "When I return, I will pay for any expenses you have for taking care of him."

Jesus asked the leader which of the three men was a neighbor to the man who was attacked. The leader replied, "The man who showed him mercy." Jesus told the leader, "Go and show mercy to those who need it."

Joy in Finding What Is Lost

Tax collectors and sinners often gathered with Jesus, and the Pharisees and scribes were disgusted that Jesus welcomed and ate with sinners. Jesus knew what the religious men were saying and gave them two hypothetical scenarios.

> If a woman has 10 silver coins and loses one, doesn't she light a lamp, sweep the floor, and search carefully until she finds it? If you have 100 sheep and lose one of them, won't you leave the 99 and look for the one that is lost until you find it? When you find it, won't you be so happy and put it on your shoulders and take it home? In both cases, people rejoice when they find what they are looking for. God does not want to lose anybody.

The Prodigal Son

Jesus also told a long parable about a man with two sons. When the younger son asked for his inheritance in advance, the father sold enough of his estate to give him his half. The son took his money and wasted it by living recklessly. After he spent all his money, he became so poor that he took a job feeding pigs (Jews were not to touch anything related to a pig).

The son soon came to his senses and thought about his father's servants who had lots of food. Since he was starving, he decided to go back to his father and ask to be one of his servants. The father had watched for him every day after he left, hoping he would return. Many months later, the son appeared in the distance and the father recognized his walk. Filled with joy and love and not worrying how he looked to others, he ran to his son, threw his arms around him, and kissed him. (In that culture, older men never ran.) The father told his servants to put a ring on his finger, sandals on his feet, and the best robe. The largest calf was killed so they could have a feast and celebrate, for "my son was dead but is alive; he was lost and has been found."

Jesus continued with the story. The older son who came home from working in the field wondered why people were dancing to music. He was told that his brother had returned and his father had killed the largest calf to celebrate. The older brother was angry and did not join in the celebration. The father begged him to come but the older son said, "I've slaved for you all these years and never disobeyed you. You never gave me even a young goat to celebrate with my friends. But when this son of yours comes home after squandering your money in wild living, you kill the largest calf for him!"

The father said with deep love, "My son, you are always with me, and everything I have is yours. But we have to celebrate because your brother was dead and is alive again – he was lost but now he has been found."

(The term *prodigal* means spending resources freely or being wastefully extravagant. The story usually applies the term to the son, but in the context of Jesus's teachings about God's concern for the lost, the story is about the extravagant love of the father for those who don't deserve it. So "The Prodigal Father" is a better title for the story.)

More Examples of Unexpected Generosity

When Jesus was invited to dinner by a well-respected Pharisee and many of his friends, he told a parable about a man who prepared a lavish dinner for many invited guests. When dinner was ready, he had his servant tell all who were invited to come. But they all had excuses for not coming, and the servant told the man that nobody was coming. The man was angry and told his servant to go into the streets and alleys and bring in the poor, the crippled, the blind, and the lame. The servant did it, but there was still room for more guests. The host then told the servant to go into the entire region to get more people, and his house was filled.

Jesus told another group of people a parable about how God would be generous to those who don't deserve it. The coming kingdom would be like a landowner who went out early in the morning and hired workers for his vineyard, saying he would pay them one day's wage for one day of work. But a few hours later, the landowner hired more people who wanted work and said he would pay them a fair wage. He did the same thing several more times, including hiring workers late in the afternoon.

At the end of the day, everybody came to be paid. The owner started with the last ones hired late in the day, and received a wage for the entire day. Those who were hired early in the morning saw this and expected to receive much more than one day's wage. But each person received the same amount, a day's wage, regardless of how many hours they worked.

Those who were hired first began grumbling and told the owner that it wasn't fair that those who worked only one hour got the same pay, even though others did most of the work. But the owner said he wasn't being unfair. He paid them the wage he had promised. He then said, "Don't I have a right to be generous with my own money? You are jealous of my generosity! The last will be first, and the first will be last."

Forgiveness

Peter once asked Jesus how often people should forgive others. The Jewish tradition was to forgive somebody three times, and Peter suggested that the right number might be up to seven times. But Jesus said the right number was 77 times, and then told this story.

> A king was owed a very large sum of money by one of his servants. When the king came to collect, the man could not pay it. The king then ordered him, his family, and all their possessions sold to repay the debt. But the servant fell to his knees and begged for mercy, saying he would pay everything back. The king felt sorry for him and cancelled the debt and let him and his family go.
>
> But then the servant went to a man who owed him a tiny debt. When the man said he couldn't pay it back, the servant demanded the money. When the

man begged for patience, the servant had him thrown into prison until he could pay the debt.

When the other servants saw this, they told the king, who called the servant and said, "I cancelled your large debt, so you should have shown mercy to the man who owed you a small debt." The king then threw the servant who had been forgiven into jail until he could pay back what he owed.

There was no way either servant could ever pay the king what was owed. Jesus concluded by saying God would not forgive those who did not forgive others. Jesus implied that we should always forgive those who ask for it.

Parables about Soils and Seeds

As Jesus traveled in the region, he spoke good news about the kingdom of God and told this parable.

A farmer scattered his seeds, and some fell on the path where they were walked on and eaten by birds. Other seeds fell on rocky ground, and when they sprouted, the plants withered because they had no moisture. Other seeds fell among thorns that choked the plants. But other seeds fell on good soil, and they grew up and produced a huge crop.

His disciples asked him to explain what the parable meant. Jesus said:

The seeds are the word of God. The seeds on the path are those who hear, but the devil comes and takes away the word from their hearts, so they do not believe. The seeds on the rocky ground are those who receive the word with joy, but they have no roots – when things get hard, they fall away. The seeds that fell in the thorns are those who hear, but they are choked by life's worries, riches, and pleasures and don't mature in their faith. But the seeds on good soil are those with good hearts, who hear the word and keep it, and produce a good crop because of their perseverance.

Jesus told another story about the kingdom of God. It was like the seeds scattered on the ground. Over time, the seeds somehow grow. All by itself, the soil gradually produces grain, which is harvested when it is ready. The kingdom is also like invisible yeast that mysteriously makes bread rise.

The Sermon on the Mountain

Jesus sometimes spoke to thousands of people at a time. Once he spoke for a very long time on a mountain to several thousand people. Some of what he preached was hard to understand and was different from what had been taught before.

Blessed are the poor in spirit, for theirs is the kingdom of heaven.

Blessed are those who are sad, for they will be comforted.

Blessed are the humble, for they will inherit the earth.

Blessed are those who hunger and thirst to live correctly, for they will be filled.

Blessed are those who are kind, for they will be shown kindness.

Blessed are those who have good thoughts and desires, for they will see God.

Blessed are the peacemakers, for they will be called children of God.

Blessed are those who are persecuted because they live the right way, for theirs is the kingdom of heaven.

Blessed are you when people are mean to you and say all kinds of false and evil things against you because of me. Rejoice and be glad, for your reward will be great in heaven, for they persecuted the prophets who came before you.

You are the salt of the earth and the light of the world. A town built on a hill can't be hidden. People don't light a lamp and hide it – they put it on its stand where it gives light to everyone. Let your light shine so others see your good deeds and glorify God.

I haven't come to get rid of the Law or the words

of the Prophets – I came to fulfill them. It was written long ago, "You shall not murder, and anyone who murders will be judged." But I say that anyone who is angry with a brother or sister will be judged. If you are offering a gift at the altar and remember that your brother or sister has something against you, go be reconciled to them and then come back and give your gift.

It was written long ago, "You shall not commit adultery." But I tell you that anyone who looks at a person and wants them for themselves has committed adultery in their heart. If your right eye causes you to stumble, cut it out.

It's been said that you should take an eye for an eye and a tooth for a tooth. But I say, if anyone slaps you on the right cheek, turn your other cheek to them. If anyone forces you to go one mile, go two miles for them. Give to those who ask and don't turn away from those who want to borrow from you.

It's been said that you should love your neighbor and hate your enemy. But I say, love your enemies and pray for those who are mean to you. If you love those who love you, that's nothing – even the tax collectors do that!

Don't practice your religion for others to see. When you give to the needy, don't make it obvious as religious people do so they get praised by others. When you give, do it in secret. God sees what is done in secret and will reward you.

Don't try to get lots of nice things for yourselves, because they can be destroyed or stolen. Instead, do nice things for others, which can't be destroyed or stolen. Don't worry about your life or your body and what you will wear. Look at the birds – they don't store food in barns, yet God feeds them. You are far more valuable than birds. Worrying can't make your life a single hour longer. Instead, seek first God's kingdom and do what is right, then everything will be given to you. Don't worry about tomorrow – there's plenty of trouble to deal with each day.

Don't judge others, for you will be judged in the way you judge others. Why do you look at the tiny bit of dust in another person's eye but ignore the log in your own eye? First take the log out of your own eye, and then you will see clearly so you can remove the tiny bit of dust from the other's eye.

Do to others what you would have them do to you – this sums up the Law and the Prophets. The gate and road that lead to destruction are wide, but the gate and road that lead to life are narrow. Take the narrow road and use the narrow gate. Few people take that route – most follow false leaders who look peaceful but are like wolves on the inside. You will know them by their fruit. Do people pick grapes or figs from plants with thorns? Every good tree bears good fruit, but a bad tree bears bad fruit. Every tree that doesn't bear good fruit is cut down and thrown into the fire. So not everyone who calls me "Lord" will enter the kingdom of heaven, but only those who do the will of my God in heaven. Many will say to me on that day, "Lord, didn't we teach in your name and perform many miracles?" I'll tell them, "I never knew you. Get away from me, you evildoers!"

Those who put my words into practice are like the wise who built their house on a rock. The rains came and the winds blew and beat against that house. But it didn't fall because its foundation was solid. But those who hear my words and don't practice them are like fools who built their house on sand. The rains came and the winds blew and beat against that house, and it washed away.

Prayer

Jesus taught about how to speak to God. Those who pray shouldn't use flowery language so they can impress others, and they shouldn't say the same things over and over again. Instead, people should pray in private and be honest, telling God their deepest thoughts and feelings. God knows what people need even before they ask for it.

Jesus provided a sample prayer that contained certain basic elements. These included (1) a recognition that God is holy, (2) a desire for the kingdom of God to influence this world so it becomes more like heaven, (3) asking for the basic necessities we need to survive, (4) asking for forgiveness for our sins and for help to forgive others, and (5) seeking protection from evil forces in the world. Prayers can focus on praise, thanksgiving, and requests. Jesus said God loves it when people pray and wants everybody to depend on God to have their needs met.

> Everyone who asks will receive, those who seek will find, and those who knock will have the door opened. Which of you, if your children ask for bread, will give them a stone? If those who are evil know how to give good gifts to their children, how much more will God give good gifts to those who ask!

Jesus often retreated into quiet and private places to be alone and talk with God. There was no specific time or place when he prayed – his awareness of God was constant and continual, and listening to God through silence was part of the process.

God Is Revealed in Jesus

Jesus referred to God as his Father.

> Everything has been given to me by my Father. Nobody knows the Father except the Son and those he chooses. Come to me if you are weary and burdened and I will give you rest. Let me guide you like a farmer guides an ox by wearing a yoke. My yoke is easy, my burden is light. If you know me, you know God; you will know the truth, and it will set you free. I am gentle and humble, and your spirit will find rest.

The disciples asked Jesus what sign he would give to help them believe him – they said the Israelites were given manna, bread from heaven. Jesus told them, "God is the one who gives you the true bread from heaven. I am the bread of life; my body is the bread I give the world. Those who believe in me will not be hungry or thirsty. I won't drive away anybody who comes to me."

Some Jews grumbled when he said he came from heaven. They knew him as a child of Joseph and Mary, so how could he say he came from heaven? The Jews also wondered how Jesus could give them his body to eat. Jesus told them, "Unless you eat the flesh of the Son of Man and drink his blood, you don't have life in you. Those who eat my flesh and drink my blood have eternal life – I will raise them up on the last day."

After hearing this, many who took his words literally left him. Jesus asked his 12 disciples if they wanted to leave him, but Simon Peter said, "Lord, who else should we follow? You have the words of eternal life. We know you are the Holy One of God."

The Costs of Discipleship

Jesus wanted the people who followed him to think carefully about being his disciples. He told them, "If someone comes to me but loves their family or their own life more, they can't be my disciple." Then he told several stories to explain what he meant.

> If you want to build a tower, you first estimate the cost to see if you have enough money to complete it? If you start but can't finish it, everyone will ridicule you. Or if a king is thinking about going to war, won't he first think about if his army can defeat an army twice the size? I send you out like sheep among wolves, so be on your guard. You must be as wise as snakes but also innocent like a dove. You will be handed over to the authorities and whipped in synagogues. You will be brought before many leaders and Gentiles to be my witnesses. But when they arrest you, don't worry about what to say or how to say it – God's Spirit will speak through you. You will be hated by everyone because of me, and when you are persecuted, flee to another place. Don't be afraid of those who kill the body – they can't kill the spirit. But watch out for those who are evil who want to take you with them to hell. I will acknowledge to God in heaven those who speak for me, but I will disown those who disown me

to others. Whoever loses their life for my sake will find it.

Preparing for Judgment

Jesus told several parables about being ready and prepared for God's return and the judgment of all people. He first spoke about 10 virgins who were waiting to meet their bridegroom at an unknown time. Five were foolish – they had lamps to light the night but didn't have oil to refill their lamps. The other five were wise – they had lamps and kept oil to refresh them. After waiting a long time, they all fell asleep. When the bridegroom arrived in the middle of the night, the foolish women couldn't light their lamps, and the wise women wouldn't share their oil. When the foolish women went to buy oil, the bridegroom came and took the wise women to the wedding banquet. When the foolish women came later with their oil, the bridegroom said he didn't know who they were. Jesus ended this parable by saying people should be prepared because the time of judgment is not known.

Parable of the Gifts of Gold

Jesus also told a story about making wise use of what we have while we are alive. He described three servants who were given various amounts of gold to use while the owner was away on a long journey. The owner gave gold to each based on their ability to use it wisely. One servant got five bags, one servant got two bags, and the third got one bag.

The servant who got five bags of gold used it wisely and earned five more bags of gold. The servant who received two bags also used the gold wisely and doubled the amount of gold. But the servant who had been given one bag dug a hole and hid the gold in the ground.

When the owner returned and asked for the gold, the servants who had been given five and two bags presented the owner with double the amount they were given. The owner said to them, "Well done, good and faithful servant!

You have been faithful with a few things; I will put you in charge of many things. Come share in my happiness!"

The servant who was given one bag of gold told the owner that he was afraid and buried the gold in the ground, and he gave the owner the bag. The owner said to this servant, "You are wicked and lazy! You should have at least put the gold in the bank so I could get back the gold plus interest." The owner gave the one bag of gold to the servant who had 10 bags and said that those who use what they have will be given more, but those who don't use what they have will lose what they have. Then the owner had the last servant thrown into the darkness where people weep.

Parable of the Sheep and the Goats

Jesus told a parable to describe who would go to heaven and who would go to hell. He said the king will sit on a throne, and as each person stands before him, he will separate them like a shepherd separates sheep from goats. The king will say to some, "Come into the kingdom, for I was hungry and you gave me something to eat, I was thirsty and you gave me a drink, I was a stranger and you welcomed me, I needed clothes and you clothed me, I was sick and you looked after me, I was in prison and you visited me."

But these people will ask the king, "When did we see you in these ways and respond the way you say we did?" The king will say to them, "When you did these things to my brothers and sisters, you did it to me."

Then the king will say to the others, "You are cursed and will go into the eternal fire prepared for the devil and his angels. For I was hungry, thirsty, a stranger, without clothes, and sick, but you didn't help me." This group will ask in wonder about when they saw him in these ways and didn't help him. The king will tell them, "Whatever you didn't do for those who had these problems, you didn't do for me." The people in this group will go into eternal punishment, but the righteous will live forever in heaven.

Condemnation of Religious Leaders

Jesus often spoke harshly to religious leaders because they were leading the people astray, not modeling good behavior, and had mixed motives. They were confident in their own religious practices and looked down on everyone else. Jesus told this parable.

> Two men went to the Temple to pray, one a Pharisee and the other a tax collector. The Pharisee prayed loudly saying, "God, I thank you that I'm not like other people – robbers, evildoers, adulterers – or even like this tax collector. I fast twice a week and give a tenth of all I get." But the tax collector stood at a distance, beat his chest and said, "God, have mercy on me, a sinner." I tell you that this man, not the Pharisee, can go home with confidence and stand before God. All who brag about themselves will be humbled; those who humble themselves will be praised.

On several occasions, Jesus harshly criticized religious leaders in front of others. He scolded the Pharisees for giving a tenth from their garden but neglected being fair, loving kindness, and walking humbly with God. He called them hypocrites because they said they approved of what their ancestors did, but their ancestors killed the prophets. They were like white tombstones that look good on the outside but were dead and unclean on the inside.

Parable of the Vineyard

Jesus told them a parable about a landowner who planted a vineyard and buildings to protect it. Then he rented the vineyard to some farmers and left. When the harvest time approached, he sent his servants to the tenants to collect his fruit. The tenants beat one servant and killed two others. The owner sent more servants, and they were treated the same way. Finally, the owner sent his son, thinking the tenants would surely respect him. But when the tenants saw the son, they said to each other, "This is the heir. Let's kill him and take his inheritance." So they killed him as well.

Jesus asked the Pharisees what would happen when the owner of the vineyard returned. The Pharisees said, "He will destroy these evil tenants and rent the vineyard to other tenants." Jesus said to them, "The Scriptures say, 'The stone the builders rejected has become the cornerstone.' Therefore, the kingdom of God will be taken away from you and given to people who will produce fruit."

After hearing these rebukes and remembering all the other things Jesus had said to them, the Pharisees and scribes were done arguing. They wanted to arrest him, but they were afraid of the crowd because most people thought he was a prophet. They watched Jesus closely and sent spies who pretended to be sincere in order to trap him and find something he said so they could turn him in to the Roman governor. These spies questioned him: "Teacher, we know you speak what is right, that you are fair and teach the way of God. Is it right for us to pay taxes to Caesar or not?"

Jesus saw through their clever trap and asked them, "Show me a coin. Whose image and inscription are on it?"

"Caesar's," they replied.

Jesus said to them, "Give to Caesar what is Caesar's, and give to God what is God's." Amazed by his answer, they kept quiet and were not able to trap him in anything he said.

11
ARREST AND EXECUTION, THEN LIFE

In his third year of ministry, Jesus talked more often about being a servant and his own death. He had been careful when he talked about his role in the world and often spoke about himself as the Son of Man or as "he" and used symbols to say who he was. For example, he said, "I am the bread of life" and "I am the resurrection and the life – those who believe in me will live, even when they die." He silenced demons when they said he was the Messiah. He performed miracles that fulfilled the predictions about him being the Messiah, the Servant-King described by the prophets. But he told people not to talk about the miracles he did that indicated he was the Messiah because it "wasn't the right time."

The Jews were getting impatient and wanted to know if he was the Messiah. He referred to God as his Father in heaven and spoke about the kingdom of God that had come. Some were in awe of his power, but the things he said were so radically different that some wanted to stone him – it was a sin to claim to be God. To the religious leaders, Jesus was leading the Jews away from the truth.

Jesus also talked indirectly about his own death and how it would lead to eternal life in heaven. For example, he called himself "the good shepherd."

> I am the good shepherd and the gate for the sheep
> who know and listen to his voice. He knows the name
> of each one and leads them out, and they follow him.
> I am the gate – those who enter through me will be

saved and find pasture. I have come that they may have a full and abundant life! The good shepherd lays down his life for the sheep. There will be one flock and one shepherd. My Father loves me because I lay down my life. No one takes my life – I choose to lay it down.

After Jesus raised Lazarus from the dead, the chief priests and the Pharisees met with the religious leaders and discussed what they should do. They said that people would believe him if he was not stopped. They thought the Romans would take away the temple and they would lose whatever independence they had. The high priest said it was better for one man to die than to let the whole nation perish. They decided to arrest Jesus and have him killed.

Jesus Enters Jerusalem

Jesus's time had come. He went to Jerusalem with his followers for the spring Passover Festival, but before entering the city, he had two disciples get a donkey and its colt. This fulfilled what the prophet Zechariah wrote about the Messiah: "Your king comes to you, gentle and riding on a colt, the foal of a donkey."

The disciples brought him the animals and placed their coats on them for Jesus to sit on. A large crowd put their coats and branches from trees on the road as he entered the city. The crowds along the road shouted, "Hosanna to the Son of David! Blessed is he who comes in the name of the Lord!" The entire city was energized and people asked who was causing the excitement. The people said it was Jesus, the prophet from Nazareth.

The Last Meal with the Disciples

Thursday evening before Passover, Jesus knew it was time for him to leave this world and return to God in heaven. He gathered the 12 disciples together in the upper room of a friend's home for the evening meal. During the meal, Jesus took off his robe, wrapped a towel around his waist, and poured water into a large bowl. Then he washed his disciples' feet and dried them with the towel.

After Jesus washed all of their feet, he returned to the table and asked the men, "Do you understand what I have done for you? You call me 'Teacher' and 'Lord,' which are both correct. But I have washed your feet to set an example, that you should do as I have done for you."

While they ate together, Jesus passed around a loaf of bread so they could each have a piece. After saying a blessing, he took the bread and said, "This is my body, given for you. Eat it and remember me." After they ate the bread together, Jesus passed around a cup of wine and said, "Everybody drink from this cup. It is my blood that is the new covenant which is poured out for many people for the forgiveness of all their sins." (This "meal" became known as the Lord's Supper.)

During the rest of the meal, the disciples started arguing with each other about who would be in various positions of power under Jesus when he became the king. Jesus told them, "The Romans are proud and like to show their power to the Jews. But you shouldn't act like them. Instead, if you want to be great, you must serve others; those who want to be first must be a slave of all. For even the Son of Man didn't come to be served but to serve and give his life for many."

Jesus then said that one of them would betray him. His disciples were stunned and stared at each other. Jesus revealed to John that it was Judas Iscariot. After Judas took the bread, he left the room – he had made a deal with the Pharisees to have Jesus arrested that night when the crowds were not around. He offered to identify Jesus in exchange for 30 pieces of silver.

After Judas left, Jesus told the others, "I won't be with you much longer. The Son of Man will be handed over to be killed. You can't come where I'm going. But if you love me, keep my commands. And now I'm giving you a new command: Love one another in the same way I have loved you. It is by your love for each other that people will know you are my disciples. The greatest love is to sacrifice your life to save others."

Peter said he would die for Jesus, but Jesus replied, "Really? Tonight you will deny me three times before the rooster crows! You will all leave me, but after I have risen, I will go ahead of you to Galilee." He told the disciples not to worry, and then Jesus said:

> I am the way and the truth and the life. Nobody comes to the Father except through me. If you know me, you know my Father. I speak the words of the Father who lives in me and who is doing the work. Those who believe in me will do more things than what you have seen because God will give you the Spirit to help you and be with you forever. The world won't understand anything about this invisible Spirit, but it will be in you. Because I live, you will live. The Spirit will teach you all things and remind you of what I have said to you.

> I am the true vine. You are the branches and God is the gardener who cuts off dead branches and prunes the living branches so they will produce more fruit. No branch can bear fruit by itself; it must stay connected to the vine. You can't bear fruit unless you stay close to me; apart from me you can't do anything. Bear fruit to show you are my disciples. If the world hates you, remember it hated me first. In this world you will have trouble, but don't be discouraged – I have overcome the world!

The Garden of Gethsemane

They left the upper room and walked to the garden of Gethsemane just outside the city walls. Jesus was very sad and told his disciples to pray for him as he went further into the garden with Peter, James, and John. He told the three men to stay with him and watch for anything that might come their way. Then he went even further into the garden and prayed to God, "If it's possible, take this cup away from me. But do what you must, not what I want."

He returned to his three disciples several times, and each time they were sleeping, not watching. He said to Peter, "Can't you watch for one hour? The spirit is willing, but the flesh is weak." Each time Jesus retreated into the garden to be alone and prayed, "Father, if this cup can't be taken from me, I will do it." Finally, he came back to all the disciples and told them, "The hour has come. I will now be delivered to the sinners. Here comes my betrayer!"

Judas Iscariot showed up with servants of the religious leaders and many men armed with weapons because they expected a fight. Judas gave Jesus a kiss, a traditional greeting that was also a signal to the others about who they should arrest. The armed men grabbed Jesus, who asked the leaders, "Am I leading a rebellion so you have to bring swords and clubs to capture me? I sat in the Temple teaching and you didn't arrest me. But this is happening to fulfill the writings of the prophets." Seeing that Jesus had been arrested, all the disciples left quickly and quietly.

The Trial of Jesus

It was the middle of the night and Jesus was taken to meet all the members of the Sanhedrin. They were looking for solid evidence against him to justify putting him to death, but no evidence was given. Finally, two members said that Jesus claimed he would destroy the Temple of God and rebuild it in three days. The high priest asked Jesus if this was true, but Jesus was silent. The high priest asked him, "Tell us if you are the Messiah, the Son of God."

Jesus replied, "Yes, it is true." When the high priest heard this, he tore his clothes and said, "You have shown disrespect for God! We don't need any more witnesses! What should we do?" The others answered, "He must die!" They spit in his face and hit him with their fists. Others slapped and mocked him, saying, "Prophesy to us! Who hit you?"

Judas saw what was happening and realized he had done an evil thing. He brought the 30 pieces of silver to the chief priest and said he had betrayed an innocent man. When the religious leaders said they didn't care, Judas threw the coins into the Temple, left the area, and killed himself.

After Jesus was arrested, Peter followed the group at a distance. He went into the courtyard and sat with the guards to see what would happen. A servant girl came to him and said he had been with Jesus. But he denied it and went to another area to wait. Another servant girl saw him and told others that she had seen him with Jesus. But Peter denied it again and swore he didn't know who Jesus was.

A little while later, others told Peter, "I'm sure you are one of them; your Galilean accent gives you away." Peter cursed loudly and swore he didn't know the man. At that moment, a rooster crowed, and Peter remembered that Jesus said he would deny Jesus three times before the rooster crowed. He left and wept bitterly.

The Roman Trial

Early Friday morning, the religious leaders made plans to have the Romans execute Jesus. They tied him up and sent him to Pontius Pilate, the governor. Pilate asked Jesus, "Are you the king of the Jews?" Jesus said he was. Pilate asked him, "Don't you hear the charges against you?" When Jesus didn't respond, Pilate was amazed that he didn't defend himself.

It was the custom at the festival for the governor to release a prisoner chosen by the crowd. At that time, a well-known revolutionary named Barabbas was a prisoner because he had killed somebody during an uprising against the Romans. When the crowd gathered, Pilate asked them who they wanted to be released, Barabbas or Jesus. The religious leaders persuaded the crowd to ask for Barabbas and to have Jesus executed. The crowd answered, "Barabbas." Pilate then asked, "What should I do with Jesus, the one who is called the Messiah?" The crowd answered, "Crucify him!"

Pilate wondered why the crowd wanted Jesus dead. He told the crowd that they should deal with him themselves, but the religious leaders said they weren't allowed to put a man to death. The Jewish leaders insisted, "According to our Law, he must die because he said he was the Son of God."

Pilate wanted to free him because he had done nothing wrong. But the Jewish leaders said that if he let Jesus go, he was no friend of Caesar – there was only one king, and anybody who claimed to be a king opposed Caesar. They also said Jesus was not following their religion – his teachings caused people to believe different things – and they would not have sent him to Pilate if he had not done something wrong.

Pilate had Jesus questioned by Herod, the government leader over Galilee who was visiting Jerusalem. But Herod could not find anything wrong with Jesus and sent him back to Pilate, who asked the crowd again why he should be crucified, for he was an innocent man.

But the crowd kept shouting, "Crucify him." They wanted Jesus dead. Pilate was disgusted and washed his hands in front of the crowd, and said Jesus was innocent and his death was their responsibility. The people answered, "We and our children are responsible for his death."

Torture and Execution

Pilate released Barabbas and Roman soldiers took Jesus away and tortured him. They stripped him and put a robe on him, then twisted together a crown made of long thorns and pushed it on his head. They made fun of him, spit on him, beat him, and hit him on the head again and again so the thorns went deep into his head. Then they whipped him so brutally that, when they were done, he was barely recognizable.

After the whipping, Jesus had to carry a large cross through the streets. The cross was soon too heavy for him, so another man carried it the rest of the way. A large number of people followed them, including women who cried loudly for him. On a hill outside the city walls, Jesus was nailed to the cross, along with two common criminals. Huge nails were driven through his hands and feet, and the cross was lifted up high for all to see. The sign above his head said, "JESUS OF NAZARETH, THE KING OF THE JEWS" and it was written in three languages.

It was around noon when the three crosses were placed in the ground. While he hung on the cross, Jesus was offered a form of wine to ease the pain, but he refused to drink it. Some of those who passed by insulted him, saying, "You said you would destroy the Temple and build it in three days – save yourself! Come down from the cross if you are the Son of God!" The religious leaders also went up the hill and insulted him. They said to the crowd, "He saved others, but he can't save himself! If he is the king of Israel, let him come down from the cross, and then we will believe in him."

One of the two men being crucified next to him also insulted Jesus, saying, "If you are the Messiah, save yourself and us!" But the other criminal said, "We are getting what we deserve, but this man did nothing wrong." Then he asked Jesus to remember him. Jesus replied, "Truly, you will be with me in paradise today."

Many of his followers watched from a distance. Some expected a miracle to happen. His mother, his aunt, Mary Magdalene, and John were at the foot of the cross, and as Jesus hung there, he told John to take care of his mother. He also said to God, "Forgive all of them, for they don't know what they are doing."

The Death and Burial of Jesus

The skies turned dark for three hours after the crosses were put into the ground. At three in the afternoon, Jesus cried out in a loud voice, "My God, why have you left me?" Shortly after that, he said, "It is finished. God, I give you my spirit." At that point, the earth shook, the skies stormed, and the thick curtain of the Temple was torn in two from top to bottom. Those who were watching cried and left the scene in sad agony.

It was getting late on Friday and the Jewish leaders didn't want bodies left hanging during the Sabbath. They asked Pilate to have the men's legs broken so they would die faster and the bodies could be taken down. Soldiers broke the legs of the two men beside Jesus, but they saw Jesus was dead, so they didn't break his legs. Instead, a soldier stabbed Jesus's side, and out came a mixture of blood and water (this proved he was dead). These things fulfilled two predictions about the Messiah: "None of his bones will be broken," and "They will look at the one they pierced."

As evening approached, a rich man got permission to take Jesus's body to a new tomb that had been cut into a wall of rock in a garden. Nicodemus, the man who visited Jesus at night, went to help bury Jesus. After Jesus's body was wrapped with spices in strips of clean linen, a big stone was put in front of the tomb entrance as several women sat and watched – they wanted to see where Jesus was buried so they could come back after the Sabbath and anoint the body. He was 33 years old when he died, and his ministry had lasted only three years.

On the Sabbath, the religious leaders told Pilate that Jesus said he would rise from the dead on the third day (Sunday). In order to make sure the disciples wouldn't steal the body and say he was alive again, they asked for Roman guards to protect the tomb. Pilate ordered guards to make sure nobody disturbed the tomb, and a seal was put on the stone to make sure it stayed closed. Soldiers then guarded the tomb.

Jesus Returns from the Grave

Just before dawn Sunday morning, several women went to the tomb to cover Jesus's body with spices. It had been about 40 hours since he died Friday afternoon, and they wondered how they would roll away the stone. But when they got to the tomb, the stone had been rolled away. They entered the tomb but didn't find the body. An earthquake occurred that morning and angels rolled back the stone. The guards were so afraid that they ran away.

The women were confused when two men in bright clothes came to the tomb. They asked why they were looking for the dead and said Jesus was alive! The disciples had been told, "The Son of Man must be delivered into the hands of sinners, be crucified, and on the third day be raised again."

Mary Magdalene was one of the women who went to the tomb, and she began crying because she couldn't find Jesus. A man came up to her and asked her why she was crying. She told the man, "They have taken my Lord away, and I don't know where he is." She thought he was the gardener and asked him to tell her where the body was.

Jesus then said, "Mary," and she recognized his voice. She cried and hugged him passionately, and she knew he wasn't a ghost. He told her to tell the disciples that he was alive and would see them in Galilee.

The women ran to tell the disciples that Jesus was alive, and Mary said she had seen him. The disciples didn't believe them – what they said didn't make any sense. Peter and John ran to the tomb, and they saw strips of linen lying by themselves in the tomb but didn't see Jesus, so they didn't know what happened.

Several Roman guards told the religious leaders about the angels rolling away the stone. The soldiers were given a large bribe and told to say the disciples stole the body at night while they slept. Since Roman soldiers would be executed if they were found sleeping on the job or if they left their post, the Jewish leaders promised to bribe the governor if he found out what happened. The soldiers took the money and told the lie to others, and the story about how the disciples stole the body was spread among the Jews.

Sightings of Jesus

Later that day, two men who had followed Jesus were walking to Emmaus, a village near Jerusalem. Jesus started walking with them, but the men didn't recognize him. Jesus asked them what they were talking about. They looked down sadly, and they were surprised that Jesus didn't know what had happened in Jerusalem the past few days. They said the chief priests and other Jewish leaders had Jesus of Nazareth killed by the Romans. Everybody hoped he was the one who was going to save Israel from the Romans. Then they heard that some women went to the tomb but didn't find his body and that angels said Jesus was alive. Some of their friends also found the tomb empty.

Jesus said to them, "Remember the prophets said the Messiah had to suffer these things before entering his glory?" He then explained what all the scriptures said about himself, all the way back to Moses.

As they entered Emmaus, the two men urged him to stay with them because it was getting dark. Jesus went with them, and when they saw his wounded hands as he broke bread, they realized who he was.

But suddenly he was gone. They told each other how inspired they felt as they walked with him while he explained the scriptures to them. They immediately went back to Jerusalem and found 10 disciples (Thomas was not there) and said they had seen Jesus.

Jesus Appears to the Disciples

That night, the disciples were hiding together because they were afraid the Jewish leaders would come after them as well. Jesus suddenly stood among them and said, "Peace be with you!" They were surprised and afraid and thought he was a ghost. But Jesus told them, "Don't be afraid or have any doubts. Look at my hands and my feet. It's me! Touch me – a ghost doesn't have flesh and bones."

He then asked for something to eat, and he ate some fish in front of them to prove he was not a ghost. He explained the scriptures so they would see how everything made sense now that they knew he was the Messiah, the Christ:

> This is what I told you earlier: Everything must be fulfilled that was written about me in the scriptures. The Messiah had to suffer and die but would rise from the dead on the third day so all the world will know that those who repent will have their sins forgiven.

Thomas was not there and the other disciples told him later that they had seen Jesus. But Thomas didn't believe them and said he wouldn't believe them until he saw the nail marks in his hands, put his finger where the nails were, and put his hand on his side. A week later, all of the disciples were in a house with the doors locked, but Jesus came and stood with them. He turned to Thomas and said, "Put your finger here; see my hands. Reach out your hand, and put it into my side. Stop doubting and believe."

Thomas exclaimed, "My Lord and my God!" Jesus replied, "You believe because you have seen me; blessed are those who haven't seen me and still believe."

Jesus Appears in Galilee

Jesus appeared again to some of his disciples near the Sea of Galilee. They had been fishing in Peter's boat at night but caught nothing. Early that morning, Jesus stood on the shore but the disciples didn't recognize him. He called and asked if they caught anything. They said they had not caught anything. Jesus told them to throw the net on the other side of the boat, and when they did, they caught so many fish that they couldn't haul in the net.

John told Peter that it was Jesus! Peter jumped into the water and went ashore. The other disciples came to shore in the boat, towing the net full of fish. Jesus told them all to eat breakfast with him and bring some of their fish. They knew it was Jesus, and it was the third time Jesus appeared to his disciples after he came back to life.

When they finished eating, Jesus asked Peter three times if he loved him, and Peter said yes three times. Each time, Jesus told Peter to "Take care of my sheep." Peter had denied Jesus three times, but he now had confirmed his allegiance to Jesus three times.

Final Words and Actions

When the 11 disciples were in Galilee, Jesus told them, "I have been given all authority in heaven and on earth. I will always be with you, even when you die. Now go and make disciples in all the nations. Baptize them and teach them to obey everything I said to you."

When they all went to an area near Jerusalem, the disciples asked Jesus when he was going to restore the kingdom of Israel. He told them, "It's not for you to know the time or day, only God knows. But you will receive power when the Holy Spirit comes on you, and you will be my witnesses in Jerusalem, then in Judea and Samaria, and then throughout the world."

Jesus then lifted his hands, blessed them, and went up into the clouds. They watched him closely as he rose, and two men dressed in white clothes suddenly stood with them. They told the disciples that Jesus went to heaven and will come back the same way. The disciples worshipped him and returned to Jerusalem filled with joy. It had been 40 days since Jesus had risen from the dead, and more than 500 people had seen him.

When the disciples returned to Jerusalem, they were joined by others, including Jesus's mother and several women. Since Judas Iscariot was dead, Peter said he should be replaced. Two men were nominated who had been with Jesus the entire time of his ministry, from the time of John the Baptist to when Jesus ascended into the sky. In the end, Matthias was selected to replace Judas Iscariot. There were about 120 people who had faithfully followed Jesus and believed what he had said. They stayed committed to following his example and to be witnesses to what happened and what Jesus had said. (Map 8 in Appendix E shows where key events in the ministry of Jesus took place.)

* * * * *

Jesus hadn't come as a king in the usual way. His entrance in a small town in a barn foreshadowed his humility. He rarely used his unusual powers except to help others. He modeled service as he spoke mainly to the Jews – they were God's people but had misunderstood what God had tried to teach them. Jesus's actions and teachings also showed God's acceptance of all people, not just the Jews. His focus on those who were disadvantaged in some way showed a different set of priorities, and his refusal to conform to the religious rules demonstrated a new way of thinking. Love was the highest priority, not obeying rules. Loving others heals people's bodies, minds, and spirits, and sacrificial love brings peace in the human heart and harmony in our relationships with each other. In addition, the sacrifice of Jesus's blood was similar to the blood of a perfect lamb that was sacrificed by the Israelites during the Passover in Egypt – it saves all people from death.

12
THE PEOPLE RESPOND
AND SCATTER

Those who followed Jesus waited in Jerusalem for the time when they would receive God's spirit. During the Jewish festival of Shavuot (50 days after Jesus died), they were gathered in a large house when a strong wind suddenly filled the house, and something resembling tongues of fire touched each of them. They were all filled with the Holy Spirit, and each began to speak another language. (The arrival of the Spirit became known as "Pentecost.") When they went into the city, Jews who were there from Asia, Africa, and Europe were amazed to hear Galileans speaking their language and talking about the wonders of God. Those who didn't know the other languages made fun of them because they thought they were drunk.

Peter Leads as the Movement Grows

Peter addressed the crowd as the 11 other disciples stood by him. He told the Jews that those speaking what seemed like babble to them were not drunk. Instead, they were fulfilling the predictions made by the prophet Joel that God would pour out the Spirit on all people, both the young and the old, men and women. Peter told his fellow Israelites:

> Jesus of Nazareth was a man approved by God to perform various miracles and signs. It was God's plan that he was handed over by wicked men to be killed, but God raised him from the dead because it was impossible for death to hold him. God promised

King David that one of his descendants would come to the throne who would be the Messiah who died and came back to life. We all witnessed that he came back to life. Be assured of this: God made Jesus, who you crucified, both Lord and Messiah.

The people felt convicted and asked Peter what they should do. Peter replied, "Repent and be baptized in the name of Jesus Christ for the forgiveness of your sins. Then you too will receive the gift of the Holy Spirit. Save yourselves from this corrupt generation." About 3,000 people were baptized and joined the movement that day.

Peter and John later went to the Temple, and a man who was crippled from birth begged every day at the Temple gate for money. Peter told him, "I don't have silver or gold, but what I have I give to you. In the name of Jesus Christ of Nazareth, walk." He took the man's hand and helped him stand up, and the man's feet and ankles instantly became strong. He started walking and was soon jumping as he praised God.

People recognized the man as the one who begged at the Temple gate, and they were amazed to see he was walking and jumping. Peter told them, "It's not our power or godliness that made this man walk. The God of Abraham, Isaac, and Jacob has glorified Jesus, but you disowned him, even though Pilate wanted to let him go. You killed Jesus, but God raised him from the dead. We saw him alive. It was this man's faith in Jesus that made him able to walk."

Peter explained how the prophets predicted the Messiah would suffer and reminded them that Moses said the Lord will raise up a prophet and people must listen to what he says; those who don't will be completely cut off. The religious leaders arrived and arrested Peter and John and put them in jail. The leaders were angry because the two disciples were teaching that Jesus had come back to life and many who heard their message believed them. By then, the number of believers had grown to about 5,000 men (not including the women).

The next day all the religious leaders met in Jerusalem and had Peter and John brought before them. They asked them who gave them the authority to say what they were saying. Peter was filled with the Holy Spirit and told them,

> If you called us here for an act of kindness shown to a man who couldn't walk and you are asking us how he was healed, then let the people of Israel know this: It is by the name of Jesus Christ of Nazareth, who you crucified but God raised from the dead, that this man was healed. Jesus is who the Psalmist said would be "the stone you builders rejected, which has become the cornerstone." Salvation is found in nobody else, for there is no other name in this world that can save a person.

When the religious leaders realized Peter and John were disciples of Jesus, they withdrew and met privately to discuss what to do next. Everybody in Jerusalem heard how Peter healed the man. The leaders decided to order Peter and John to stop teaching about Jesus, but the two of them said they couldn't stop teaching about what they had seen and heard.

After Peter and John were released, they told the other disciples what the religious leaders said and how Peter was filled by the Spirit when he spoke. They were all amazed and praised God – they realized that the threats against them gave them an opportunity to speak boldly because the Spirit would speak for them and miracles could happen by using the name of Jesus.

The apostles performed many miracles among the people. The believers started meeting in public every day in the Temple courtyard. People in Jerusalem and nearby towns came to Peter so they would be healed. Those who believed continued to learn, had fellowship with each other, and earned a good reputation. All the believers shared everything they had, and nobody claimed their possessions as their own – there were no needy people among them. When those who owned land or a house sold them, they brought the money and it was distributed to anyone who needed it.

One couple sold some property but lied about the sale price so they could keep some of the money for themselves. They both died immediately when Peter confronted them with their lie. Fear spread among the people who heard this.

The Believers Are Persecuted

The religious leaders were threatened by this new religious movement, so they arrested the apostles and put them in jail. But during the night, an angel opened the jail doors. The apostles escaped, and in the morning, they went back to the Temple to continue teaching. When the religious leaders gathered to talk to the apostles, the jailers said they were gone, and the leaders were told they were back at the Temple. The captain of the Temple guard brought the apostles to appear before the Sanhedrin to be questioned. The high priest said, "We gave you strict orders not to teach about Jesus, but you continue with your teaching and say we are responsible for his death."

Peter replied: "We must obey God, not human orders. You killed Jesus but the God of our ancestors raised him from the dead. God exalted him as Prince and Savior so he might bring Israel to repentance and forgive our sins."

The men in the Sanhedrin were furious and wanted to kill all of them. But a well-respected Pharisee named Gamaliel told the Sanhedrin to be careful when dealing with Peter and the others. He said, "You know two men who had followers and led rebellions, and they were killed. Their followers dispersed and nothing came of it. I advise you to leave these men alone. If their actions are not from God, they will fail. But if they are from God, you won't be able to stop them because you will be fighting against God."

His speech persuaded the others to release the apostles after they were whipped and ordered not to speak about Jesus. The apostles left and rejoiced because they were worthy of suffering disgrace in Jesus's name. They continued teaching and saying that Jesus was the Messiah.

The number of disciples in Jerusalem increased rapidly, and a large number of priests also started following Jesus. As the number of disciples increased, those who spoke Greek complained that their widows were being overlooked when food was distributed. The 12 apostles decided that people should be selected to lead the work to help Greek-speaking Jews who needed help. Seven "deacons" were selected to oversee the help.

Stephen Is Killed

Stephen was one of the deacons and performed many miracles, but the synagogue leaders who served Jews in Africa and Asia Minor (modern day Turkey) were angry with him. They accused him of speaking disrespectfully about Moses and God. When Stephen was taken to the Sanhedrin and asked if the charges were true, he gave a long speech about the entire history of the Israelites, all the way back to when God chose Abraham to move to Canaan. This showed that he was an educated and sincere religious man, but he then accused the religious leaders of being just like their ancestors who rejected God – they were responsible for killing Jesus, the Messiah.

Those in the Sanhedrin were furious. Stephen was filled with the Spirit and gazed into the sky and said, "I can see into heaven and Jesus is standing right next to God." When the religious leaders heard this, they covered their ears, screamed at him, and dragged him out of the city where they stoned him to death. While Stephen was being stoned, he asked God not to hold it against them. He was the first follower of Jesus to be martyred.

The Believers Scatter as Saul Leads the Persecution

Right after Stephen was killed, many followers of Jesus in Jerusalem were threatened with death. They thought Jesus was coming back very soon to establish the kingdom of God on earth and be a political king who would free them from Roman oppression, so they had all stayed close to Jerusalem. But the threat of death drove most of them into Judea and Samaria.

One of the men who watched Stephen being stoned and approved of his execution was a man named Saul. His father was a Pharisee and he was well trained in all the Jewish scriptures. He disrupted meetings of believers by going from house to house and putting them in prison. Saul threatened all the disciples of "the Way," a term given to this new religious movement because Jesus said he was "the way, the truth, and the life." Saul got letters from the high priest to take to the synagogues of Damascus so if he found anybody who belonged to the Way there, he could bring them back to Jerusalem as his prisoners.

Saul took the letters and started his trip to Damascus. When he was close to the city, a light from the sky suddenly flashed around him. He fell to the ground and heard a voice that said, "Saul, why are you persecuting me?" He asked who it was, and the voice said, "I am Jesus, the one you are persecuting. Get up and go to Damascus where you will be told what you must do." The men traveling with Saul also heard the voice. Saul got up but was now blind.

Saul's men led him into Damascus where a disciple named Ananias had a vision in which God told him to go to a house on the main road and ask for a man named Saul who was praying. Saul had a vision that Ananias would come to restore his sight. Ananias was scared – he had heard how Saul was hunting Jesus's followers and arresting them. But God told Ananias, "Go, I have chosen this man to be my instrument to preach about me to the Gentiles and the people of Israel."

When Ananias found Saul, he put his hands on him and told him, "Jesus told me to come so you will see again and be filled with the Holy Spirit." Immediately, something like scales fell from Saul's eyes and he could see. He got up and was baptized – his eyes were literally and figuratively opened. He was no longer blind, and he now understood that Jesus was the Messiah.

Saul spent several days with the disciples of the Way in Damascus. He began preaching in the synagogues that Jesus was the Messiah and the Son of God. People knew how he threatened believers in Jerusalem and were amazed at what he was saying. He grew increasingly powerful and impressed the Jews living in Damascus and proved to them that Jesus was the Messiah.

But eventually the Jews in Damascus plotted to kill Saul. They watched for him at the city gate so they could catch him, but Saul found out about the plot and escaped from the city when his followers lowered him in a basket through an opening in the wall at night. Saul went into the desert and spent three years developing his understanding of the scriptures with what he learned about Jesus.

Saul eventually returned to Jerusalem and tried to join the disciples, but they were all afraid that it was a trick for him to capture all of them at once. But Barnabas told the apostles what happened to Saul on the road to Damascus and that he was now preaching fearlessly about Jesus. Saul then stayed with them and moved freely in Jerusalem, speaking boldly and debating Hellenistic Jews. These Jews tried to kill him, but he escaped and went to his home in Tarsus (close to Adana in Turkey).

Philip

The disciples preached about Jesus wherever they went. Philip went to a city in Samaria, and people listened closely and watched him perform miracles. He delivered people from their evil spirits and healed many who could not walk. The apostles in Jerusalem heard that the Samaritans had accepted the word of God. Peter and John went to the area and placed their hands on the new believers, and they received the Spirit. Peter and John also preached in many other Samaritan villages.

An angel told Philip to take a trip south on the desert road that runs from Jerusalem to Gaza. On his way, he met an official from Ethiopia who was in charge of his queen's money. The man had been to Jerusalem to worship and was going home. As the man sat in his chariot reading the book written by Isaiah, Philip saw what the man was reading and asked him if he understood it. The man didn't understand it and invited Philip into his chariot to explain the part that said, "He was led like a sheep to the slaughter, as a lamb before its shearer is silent. He was humiliated and deprived of justice, and his life was taken from the earth."

Philip explained that the passage was about Jesus and who Jesus was and how he fulfilled Isaiah's predictions. As they traveled, they came to some water and the man stopped his chariot and had Philip baptize him. Philip then went to preach the good news in many towns, all the way north to the port city of Caesarea in Phoenicia.

Peter Continues to Lead

Meanwhile, Peter traveled around the region preaching and performing miracles. He healed a paralyzed man who lived in Lydda who had been in bed for eight years. In Joppa, a disciple named Dorcas who was always doing good and helping the poor had died. Peter found out about it and went to Joppa and met many people who had been helped by Dorcas. He went into the room where she was dead and he prayed. Then he told her to get up, and she opened her eyes and stood up with Peter's help. He then presented her to the people who were grieving her death. Word spread quickly through the town about what happened, and many more people believed in Jesus.

The Encounter with Cornelius

A Roman centurion named Cornelius was living in Caesarea with his God-fearing family. He prayed to God regularly and gave generously to those in need. One day an angel told him to send some men to Joppa and bring back a man named Peter who was staying at the home of a man named Simon. Cornelius sent several men to Joppa to find Peter.

While the men traveled to Joppa, Peter was praying and fell into a trance. He saw a large square sheet coming down from heaven, and it held all kinds of animals, including reptiles and birds, that were considered unclean. A voice told him to kill them and eat. But Peter had never eaten anything he was taught not to eat, so while he was still in the trance, he said he would not eat it. But the voice spoke again: "Don't call anything unclean that God says is clean." This happened three times, and then the sheet went back to heaven.

Peter came out of his trance and was thinking about what the vision meant when the men sent by Cornelius arrived. The Spirit told Peter that men were looking for him and had been sent to him by God. Peter asked the men why they had come. They told Peter about Cornelius, who he was and his reputation, and how an angel told him to send them to find Peter. The next day, they all returned to Caesarea with some believers from Joppa.

When they arrived in Caesarea, Cornelius greeted them at his house, which was full of Gentiles. Peter told them, "You know that our law says Jews should not associate with or visit a Gentile. But God showed me that I should not call anyone unclean. So when you called for me, I came without doubts. Why did you ask me to come?"

Cornelius told him an angel told him that he should have Peter visit them, but he didn't know why. Peter then realized why he had the vision of the forbidden food. He told everybody, "Now I understand that God doesn't show favoritism but accepts those from every nation who do what is right. God's message was sent first to the Israelites, but Jesus taught us to tell *everybody* that he is the one God appointed as judge of all people."

While Peter was still speaking these words, the Holy Spirit came on everybody in the room. The Jews who were with Peter were amazed that the Holy Spirit had also come to the Gentiles and they spoke in foreign languages as they praised God. Peter then baptized all of them.

The believers throughout Judea heard that the Gentiles had received the good news about God. When Peter went to Jerusalem, the Jewish believers criticized him for going to a Gentile's house. But Peter told them the whole story and how the Holy Spirit came to the Gentiles. He said, "If God gave believing Gentiles the same Spirit we received, who was I to stand in God's way?" After hearing this, they didn't object anymore and praised God when they realized even the Gentiles could be saved by asking for their sins to be forgiven.

The Christians and the Church in Antioch

Those who were scattered by the persecution traveled as far as Phoenicia, Cyprus, and Antioch, spreading the word only to Jews. Some who went to Antioch told the Greeks about Jesus, and many believed. When news of this reached Jerusalem, Barnabas went to Antioch to see what was happening, then went to Tarsus to get Saul, and they both returned to Antioch. Barnabas and Saul spent one year with the followers in Antioch, and the disciples there were called "Christians" for the first time. Collectively, they were known as the "church," the term Jesus used when telling Peter that he would lead his followers.

Map 9 in Appendix E shows where the early apostles went after leaving Jerusalem.

13
PAUL'S TRIPS TO ASIA MINOR AND EUROPE

The good news about Jesus spread across the region. People were told that Jesus had died as a permanent sacrifice for the sins of the entire world, so anybody could have a relationship with a living God if they wanted it. A sign that they had changed their ways and were Christians was that they were baptized and obeyed the teachings of Jesus, including loving others. Peter led the teaching of the Jews in Judea and Samaria. A Christian named Mark became close to Peter and wrote a short book about the life of Jesus. At the same time, the church with many Gentiles in Antioch grew under the leadership of Saul, Barnabas, and others. Saul was referred to as Paul, his Greek name.

Paul and Barnabas Take Their First Trip

About 20 years after Jesus had gone to heaven and after spending five years in Antioch, Paul and Barnabas took a trip to preach elsewhere. They sailed to Cyprus where Paul preached in the synagogues, and then sailed to Perga (in southern Turkey) and went 100 miles north to Pisidian Antioch in the Galatian region of Asia Minor.

Paul spoke in the synagogue on the Sabbath about the history of the Israelites and the prophecies about the Messiah. Then he talked about Jesus, that he was a descendant of David and the Messiah. Although Jesus had been killed, he came back to life and lived for many days and many people saw him. What God promised to their

Jewish ancestors had been fulfilled: through Jesus, sins were forgiven, and through him everyone who followed him was set free from every sin—this could not be done under the laws of Moses.

The people invited Paul and Barnabas to come back the next week, and almost the entire city gathered to hear them speak. When the Jewish leaders saw the crowd, they were jealous and started debating Paul and verbally abused him. Paul and Barnabas responded boldly: "We had to speak to the Jews first. But since you reject what we have said and don't want eternal life, we now turn to the Gentiles. The Lord told us that we are a light to the Gentiles so the entire world can be saved." The Gentiles were glad to hear this and felt honored by God, and many of them became Christians. But the Jewish leaders arranged to have Paul and Barnabas expelled from the area. As they left, the two men shook the dust off their feet and went to Iconium, a city 75 miles away.

Preaching in Iconium, Lystra, and Derbe

In Iconium, Paul and Barnabas went to the synagogue first and spoke so well that many Jews and Greeks believed their message. But again, many Jewish leaders refused to believe and got others to accuse them of telling lies. Paul and Barnabas spent many days preaching boldly and performing miracles, and the people of Iconium were divided – some sided with the Jews while others believed the two apostles. A plot developed to kill the two men, but they found out about it and escaped to Lystra, a city 20 miles away.

Paul and Barnabas preached in Lystra and the nearby area. They met a man who had never walked, and Paul looked at him and said his faith had healed him. When he told the man to stand up, the man jumped up and started walking.

When the crowd saw what Paul did, they shouted, "The gods have come to us in human form!" They thought they were the Roman gods, Zeus and Hermes, but the two apostles shouted, "We are human like you. We have good news – turn from these worthless gods and follow the living

God, the one who made the heavens and earth, the sea and everything in them. Until now, God has let everybody go their own way, but God still showed kindness by giving you rain and crops so you would have food."

Jews who had come from Pisidian Antioch and Iconium turned the crowd against them. They stoned Paul and dragged him outside the city, thinking he was dead. But some disciples took him back into the city. The next day he and Barnabas left for Derbe, where they preached and many people believed. Then they went back the way they had come, strengthening the believers in each city.

They returned to Perga and sailed back to Antioch and told the believers there what happened on their trip. They were gone two years and the Christians were happy to hear that more Gentiles were now disciples.

The Council at Jerusalem

Some disciples came from Judea to visit the church in Antioch. They had been teaching that new Gentile believers had to be circumcised in order to be saved, but Paul and Barnabas disagreed. They took a small group of church leaders from Antioch to visit the Christian leaders in Jerusalem to discuss the issue. Everybody listened as Paul and Barnabas talked about what God had done among the Gentiles they met in Asia Minor.

Some believers who were Pharisees said the Gentiles had to be circumcised as required by the laws of Moses. Everybody discussed the issue, and finally Peter spoke.

> Brothers, you know God has allowed Gentiles to become disciples and have the Holy Spirit. God knows our heart and doesn't see a difference between Jews and Gentiles: we can all have faith. Why should we add more rules for the Gentiles that we had a hard time following? No! We believe it is through the free gift from Jesus that we are saved. It doesn't matter how we look; it's the heart that matters.

James then spoke about how the prophet Amos wrote that "all the people of the world will seek the Lord, even the Gentiles." He said it should not be difficult for Gentiles to turn to God and they should be told not to eat food offered to idols, not to commit sexual immorality, not to eat the meat of strangled animals, and not to drink blood. Everybody agreed and wrote a letter that listed only these requirements for the Gentile believers in other regions.

Paul Takes Another Trip

A few months later, Paul and Barnabas went back to the cities they had visited in Asia Minor to see how the churches were doing. They decided to split up: Barnabas took a man named Mark who was with them on their first trip, and Paul took Silas, a man he met at the meeting in Jerusalem.

Paul and Silas traveled back to Asia Minor and strengthened the churches as they went. Paul met a disciple named Timothy whose mother was a Jewish believer but whose father was Greek. The believers in the cities respected him, and Paul invited him to join them on the trip. Timothy was circumcised in order to please the Jews in the area, and as they traveled from town to town, they told the church about what the Christian leaders in Jerusalem said about the few things they needed to do. The number of believers grew and their faith deepened.

Traveling to Macedonia

As the men traveled, the Holy Spirit had them avoid some areas, and they ended up in the port city of Troas and met a Gentile believer named Luke, a doctor, who started traveling with them. Paul had a vision of a man of Macedonia (northern Greece) begging him to come help him. Paul believed this was a call from God to go to Macedonia, so the four men (Paul, Silas, Timothy, and Luke) traveled to Philippi, a Roman colony and a major city in Macedonia.

In Philippi, they met a woman named Lydia, the owner of a large business. She worshipped God and responded to

Paul's message about Jesus. When she and the members of her household were baptized, she spent more time with the men learning about her new faith.

Paul and Silas in a Philippian Prison

The men met a female slave who worked as a fortune-teller. She followed the men for many days, shouting, "These men are servants of the highest God and are telling people how to be saved." Paul got so annoyed with her that he said to her spirit, "In the name of Jesus Christ, I order you to come out of her!" An evil spirit immediately left her.

When her owners realized the woman could no longer tell fortunes and make money for them, they dragged Paul and Silas to the local Roman officials and said the men were Jews and caused problems in the city. The officials ordered the two men stripped and beaten, and then they were put in chains in a cell deep inside the jail.

Paul and Silas were praying and singing hymns to God during the night and other prisoners were listening to them. Suddenly a violent earthquake shook the jail. All the jail doors flew open and everyone's chains came loose. The jailer woke up, and when he saw the jail doors open, he was going to kill himself because he thought the prisoners had escaped.

But Paul shouted, "Don't hurt yourself! We are all still here!" The jailer rushed in and asked Paul and Silas what he must do to be saved. They told him, "Believe in the Lord Jesus, and you and your household will be saved." The jailer washed the wounds from their beatings, took them to his house, and fed them. He and his entire household were baptized and were filled with joy because they all finally believed in the true God.

When Paul and Silas were released in the morning, Paul told the officials that they had been beaten publicly and jailed without a trial, even though they were Roman citizens. When the officials heard Paul and Silas were Roman citizens, they were alarmed and asked them to leave the city. But Paul and Silas went to Lydia's house where they were encouraged by other Christians.

In Thessalonica and Berea

Paul, Silas, and Timothy then traveled about 95 miles to Thessalonica (Luke stayed in Philippi). They went to the synagogue on three straight Sabbath days to explain the Scriptures and prove Jesus was the Messiah. Some of the Jews and many religious Greeks became Christians, including many prominent women.

But other Jews were jealous. As in other cities, they had evil men from the market form a mob and search for them. The mob went to the house where the apostles had stayed, but when they were not there, the mob dragged the owner and other believers out of the house and said they denied that Caesar was the king. When the city officials heard this, all those Christians were thrown in jail. (They were released after they paid a fine.)

To keep the apostles safe, believers took the three men to the nearby city of Berea where there was another synagogue. The Berean Jews were smarter than the people in Thessalonica and listened closely to Paul. They carefully examined the Scriptures to see if what Paul said was true, and as a result, many of them believed, as did many Greek men and a number of prominent Greek women.

But some Jews in Thessalonica heard Paul was preaching in Berea, and they came and turned the crowds against him. The believers quickly escorted Paul to Athens while Silas and Timothy stayed in Berea until they could join him safely.

In Athens

Paul was disgusted when he saw that Athens was full of idols. He preached in the synagogue and in the market, and some Greek philosophers began to debate him. Paul was invited to explain his teachings at a meeting of educated men who gathered to discuss new ideas. Paul told them, "I see you are very religious! I've walked around and seen many objects of worship and even found an altar that said, 'TO AN UNKNOWN GOD.' I'm going to talk to you about this God."

Paul reasoned with the Greek philosophers but didn't mention the Hebrew scriptures. He said that the God who made the world and everything in it didn't need to live in temples built by human hands and didn't look like the images made by humans. While God had overlooked this lack of intelligence, God now commanded everybody to repent, for someday God would judge all people. Paul was trying to convince his listeners that there was only one true God, not many gods. When he mentioned the resurrection of the dead, some in the audience sneered but others wanted to hear more. As a result, some of those who heard him became believers.

In Corinth

Paul left Athens and went to Corinth, a tough port city 30 miles away that had a reputation for immoral behavior. He met a Jewish man named Aquila who had come from Italy with his wife Priscilla because all the Jews in Rome had been ordered to leave. Paul worked and stayed with the couple who were tentmakers. (Paul then earned money to pay his travel expenses by making and selling tents.) Paul spoke in the synagogue every Sabbath and tried to persuade Jews and Greeks to become Christians. When Silas and Timothy arrived from Macedonia, Paul spent all his time preaching, and several Jewish leaders became believers. Paul stayed in Corinth for 18 months while he taught the new believers. The Roman leader in the city allowed Paul to preach, so he stayed safe from the Jews who wanted to silence him.

Paul and the others eventually sailed across the Aegean Sea to Ephesus, a major city on the western coast of Asia Minor, and Priscilla and Aquila went with them. Paul spent time in the synagogue speaking to the Jews, who wanted him to stay there. He said he had to go to Jerusalem to tell the Christian leaders about his trip, but he would return. Aquila and Priscilla stayed in Ephesus and continued teaching about Jesus. Map 10 in Appendix E shows where Paul traveled during this period.

Paul Takes a Third Trip

Paul later took a third trip through Asia Minor and visited many cities to strengthen the disciples. He was especially eager to return to Ephesus.

Ephesus

Priscilla and Aquila were glad to see Paul when he returned. They told him about a Jewish scholar named Apollos from Egypt who had been preaching and teaching about Jesus in a very accurate way, but he left to preach and teach in Greece.

Paul did what he always did: he preached first to the Jews in the synagogue. He spoke boldly for three months, but some of the Jews spoke against the Way. So Paul and some of his disciples spent two years lecturing in a public hall. Everybody who lived in the region heard Paul's message about God, and he did extraordinary miracles using God's power. Handkerchiefs and aprons that touched him were taken to the sick, and they were healed.

Some Jewish men tried to drive out evil spirits using the name of Jesus, as if the name was a magical word. They would say, "In the name of the Jesus whom Paul preaches, I command you to come out." One day an evil spirit responded to their order and said, "I know Jesus and Paul, but who are you?" The man who had the evil spirit jumped on them and beat them all so bad that they ran out of the house naked and bleeding. When people in Ephesus heard about this, they were all afraid. Many of the new believers openly confessed their sins, and some who practiced magic burned their very rare and valuable scrolls together in public. As a result, word about Jesus kept spreading.

Paul's teachings also caused an economic crisis in Ephesus. A silversmith who made silver shrines of Artemis (the local fertility goddess) brought in a lot of business for the craftsmen in the city. He called the workers together and told them that Paul's teachings had driven away much of their business. Paul said that gods made by human hands were not gods at all, and this endangered their trades and discredited Artemis. The craftsmen were furious and started shouting, "Great is Artemis of the Ephesians!"

Soon the whole city was in an uproar and people rushed into a huge outdoor theater. Paul wanted to speak to the crowd, but the disciples and some government officials who knew him didn't let him go into the theater – the mob was out of control. Thousands of people were yelling, even though most of them didn't even know why they were there. The Jews in the crowd pushed one of their leaders to the front, who motioned for silence so he could talk to the crowd. But when the crowd realized he was a Jew, they all chanted loudly in unison for almost two hours: "Great is Artemis of the Ephesians!"

Eventually, the city clerk quieted the crowd by reminding them that everybody knew that Ephesus was the guardian of the temple of Artemis and her image had fallen from heaven. (A meteorite that resembled a woman had fallen there.) The clerk told the people that their problems would be heard in court and they could press charges. After this, everybody went home or back to work.

Further Travels

After the uproar ended, Paul went to Macedonia and Greece with some disciples. He encouraged people along the way and stayed in the region for many months. In some cities, the Jews plotted against him, so he had to change his plans. He was accompanied by believers from many cities where he had preached and taught. He wanted to return to Jerusalem and didn't know what would happen when he returned. But he was convinced that prison and hardship were in his future. He knew he would never see many of his followers again. He warned them that hard times and false teachers were coming, so they needed to persevere and be wise.

Paul's third trip lasted more than three years. Rather than being a burden to those he visited, he supported himself while teaching and debating. He modeled confident humility and service, just as Jesus had done. (Map 11 in Appendix E shows where Paul went on his third trip and where he went next, as described in the next chapter.)

14
PAUL GOES TO ROME

When Paul and the others returned to Palestine, a prophet said Paul would be arrested and delivered to the Gentiles in Jerusalem. Everybody tried to convince him not to go there, but he said he was ready to be arrested and even die if it advanced the Christian movement. The group went to Jerusalem and told the church leaders about what happened during their travels. The leaders praised God and told Paul that thousands of Jews were now believers in Palestine.

Paul Is Arrested in Jerusalem

Some Jews from Asia recognized Paul in the Temple and accused him of false teaching and letting Greeks in the Temple. This wasn't true, but people dragged him out of the Temple and tried to kill him. News reached the Roman commander that the city was rioting, and he sent soldiers to calm the crowd. The commander arrested Paul and asked what he had done. People in the crowd shouted different accusations, and the commander couldn't determine the truth. Paul was sent to the barracks and the angry mob followed.

Paul got permission to speak to the crowd and started speaking in Aramaic, quieting the crowd. Paul explained his background and how he studied the scriptures while living in Jerusalem. He was as devoted to God as anybody and had persecuted those who followed the Way. He told them what happened to him on his trip to Damascus, but when he said he had been sent to the Gentiles, the people started shouting at him again and said he should be killed.

When it looked like another riot was starting, the commander sent Paul to the barracks so he could be whipped and interrogated. As the soldiers got ready to whip him, Paul asked the lead soldier, "Is it legal for you to whip a Roman citizen who has not yet been found guilty?" The soldier quickly told the commander that Paul was a Roman citizen, and after Paul explained to the commander how he was born a Roman citizen, the commander stopped the interrogation.

The commander ordered the Sanhedrin to meet so Paul could explain himself. Paul knew some of them were Sadducees and others were Pharisees, and he started by saying, "I am a Pharisee and descended from Pharisees. I stand before you today because of my hope in the resurrection of the dead."

A dispute broke out between the Sadducees, who believed there is no resurrection nor angels nor spirits, and the Pharisees who believed in these things. Some Pharisees said Paul had done nothing wrong and the dispute started getting violent. The commander ordered Paul back to the barracks, and that night, the Spirit told Paul, "Don't worry! You have spoken about me here in Jerusalem, and you will do it again in Rome."

Meanwhile, many Jews plotted to killed Paul. They had the religious leaders ask the commander to have Paul brought before the Sanhedrin again, and they planned to kill Paul on his way to the meeting. But Paul found out about the plot and told the commander, who sent Paul to Governor Felix in Caesarea along with 470 soldiers to protect him.

The Trials in Caesarea

The Jews went to Caesarea to continue their accusations against Paul. One leader said Paul was a troublemaker who created riots among Jews all over the world, and others made different accusations.

After the Jews made their case, Paul made his case. He told Felix that he worshipped in Jerusalem but didn't argue with anyone in the Temple or cause any problems in the city. There was no evidence to support the Jews' allegations, but he admitted to being a follower of the Way. Felix was familiar with the Way and ended the proceedings. Felix left Paul in prison for two years, and Paul was given some freedoms and had his friends take care of him.

Festus replaced Felix and immediately heard the accusations against Paul. The Jews wanted Paul transferred back to Jerusalem so they could kill him on the way, but Festus wanted Paul tried in Caesarea. When Festus heard the case, the Jews couldn't prove any of their accusations. Paul made his defense again, and Festus asked him if he wanted to stand trial in Jerusalem. When Paul appealed to have his case tried by Caesar, Festus told Paul that his trial would be in Rome. Festus said Paul was innocent and got confirmation from his superiors that Paul should be tried in Rome.

Paul Sails to Rome

A boat set sail for Rome with Paul, other prisoners, and some other passengers, including Luke. A Roman commander was in charge, and the boat used a route that avoided strong winds. When the northern fall winds got stronger, Paul warned the commander that it was dangerous to keep going; if it did, the ship could be destroyed. But the commander didn't listen and followed the advice of the ship's owner and captain.

They kept going and tried in vain to reach a safe harbor. The strong winds pushed the boat away from shore, and it strained from the winds and waves. The crew wrapped ropes around the boat to hold it together and threw cargo overboard to lighten the load. The storm continued to rage and the crew threw all the ship's sailing gear overboard. The storm continued for many days and the boat drifted helplessly. Everybody was seasick and couldn't eat, and everybody thought they would all die.

Paul addressed everybody on the ship and told them not to lose hope. He said an angel of his God told him that he must stand trial before Caesar and that everybody onboard would live, even though the ship would be destroyed when it went aground on an island.

The ship drifted west across the Mediterranean Sea, and one night when the sailors measured the depth of the sea, it was rapidly getting shallower. To keep the ship from crashing onto the rocks they couldn't see, they dropped all the anchors and prayed for daylight. Some sailors tried to escape in the lifeboat, but Paul told the commander that everybody had to stay on the ship in order for everybody to live. The commander listened to him and soldiers cut the ropes that held the lifeboat, which drifted away.

Just before dawn, Paul told everybody to eat. The storm had lasted 14 days and everybody was weak, and they needed their strength to survive. Paul took some bread and thanked God in front of everybody and started to eat. The others started eating and ate as much as they wanted.

Landing on Malta

When daylight came, they saw a bay with a sandy beach and decided to run the ship onto the beach. They cut the anchors loose and the boat drifted toward the beach. But it struck a sandbar and ran aground, and the pounding surf broke it into pieces.

The soldiers planned to kill the prisoners to prevent them from swimming away and escaping, but the commander wanted to spare Paul's life, so none of the prisoners were harmed. All those who could swim got to land, and the rest hung on to whatever floated until reaching land. They all made it safely to shore.

They were on the island of Malta and the islanders helped them with unusual kindness. Paul was bitten by a poisonous snake while building a fire on the beach. The islanders saw the snake hanging from his hand and said he was a murderer – they said that although he escaped from the sea, the goddess Justice would not allow him to live. But Paul flicked the snake into the fire and wasn't harmed. The people expected him to swell up or die quickly, but after a long time, nothing happened to Paul. So they changed their minds and said he was a god.

The chief official of Malta lived near the beach and welcomed the shipwreck victims in his home. His father was sick, and when Paul placed his hands on him and prayed, the father was healed. Others on the island found out what happened, and the rest of the sick people on the island came and were cured by Paul.

Paul Preaches in Rome Under Guard

Paul and the others stayed on Malta for three months, then traveled to Rome where Paul was allowed to live by himself with a soldier who guarded him. He met with the local Jewish leaders and explained why he was there; none of them knew what happened in Jerusalem. They wanted to know what he had to say about the Way – most people were talking against it.

Paul met with a larger number of Jews who lived in Rome and talked about the kingdom of God. By connecting it to the Law of Moses and what the prophets said, he tried to persuade them that Jesus was the Messiah. Some were convinced but others wouldn't believe. Paul finished by quoting the prophet Isaiah:

> Say to the people, "You keep hearing and seeing but you will not understand, for your hearts have become insensitive. Your ears can hardly hear and you have closed your eyes." Therefore, God's salvation has been sent to the Gentiles; they will listen!

Paul stayed in a rented house for two years and had many visitors. He had written a long letter to the believers in Rome when he was in Greece, so the believers in Rome knew about him. He taught boldly about God's kingdom and Jesus the Messiah, and nobody stopped him. He sent letters of encouragement to believers and their leaders in many cities he visited in Asia Minor, Macedonia, and Greece. The letters provided more instructions to the churches.

(These letters are discussed in the next chapter. Paul was released from house arrest in AD 62 and continued preaching and teaching in southern Europe and on the island of Crete. He was imprisoned again in Rome and was killed because of his faith during the reign of Nero around AD 68. His ministry lasted about 32 years.)

15
PAUL'S LETTERS OF ENCOURAGEMENT AND INSTRUCTION

During his ministry, Paul wrote letters to the churches in Rome, Corinth, Thessalonica, Philippi, Ephesus, Colossae, and the cities in the region of Galatia (Pisidian Antioch, Iconium, Lystra, and Derbe). He also wrote to Christian leaders in various cities: Timothy in Ephesus, Titus in Crete, and Philemon in Colossae. Paul may have been the author or coauthor of a long document written to Jews ("Hebrews" is summarized in the next chapter).

The letters at that time were written on sheets of papyrus that were about the size of paper used now. Most of the time, only one sheet was used for a letter. When longer letters were written, they were connected to each other and rolled into a scroll. Sometimes scribes wrote the letters as they were dictated by the author. Long letters may have had multiple scribes.

The letters usually began with a greeting that included the name of the person sending the letter and who was to receive them. The letters usually ended with a farewell and sometimes had a message for people the author knew. Dates were not included and the letters were delivered using travelers who were known by the sender and receiver.

Religious ideas, teachings about correct living, and practical advice were usually included in Paul's letters. He described and interpreted Jesus's teachings and actions, and he discussed what they meant for believers. He also encouraged those who received the letters because they were suffering because of their new faith. Paul wrote some very long letters that included many concepts about God as he clarified and defended the faith using logical arguments.

This chapter summarizes the main messages of Paul's letters in the order they were probably written.

Letter to the Galatians

The first letter Paul wrote was to the churches in Galatia and discussed controversies about how a Christian is identified. Gentiles had joined the church, and some Jews believed they should obey all the rules of Judaism, including its food restrictions, circumcision, sacrifices, and separating from others who did not share their beliefs. In the past, Gentiles who converted to Judaism were required to follow the laws of Moses. However, most Gentiles who were becoming Christians did not want to convert to Judaism in addition to following Jesus, and many of them were leaving the church. What made a person a Christian? Was it following the ways of Jesus alone, or must they also follow the rules of Judaism?

Paul used his own experiences to say that following Jesus was enough. God's grace didn't come to him because he was a devout Pharisee who obeyed Jewish laws. Paul knew Peter had met with Gentiles and that "unclean" foods were edible for Christians. Peter approved having Paul preach to the Gentiles and stressed only the need to continue helping the poor. Paul accepted everybody because God no longer showed favoritism toward the Jews. Here is his basic argument:

> A person is not justified (declared righteous and acceptable to God) by following the law, but by faith in Jesus, the Christ. Nobody is made right by obeying the law. I died to the law so that I can live for God – I am a new person because he lives in me. I live by faith in the Son of God who loved me and gave himself for me. If righteousness can be earned through the law, Christ died for nothing. The law held us together until Jesus came and saved us; having the law proved

that we couldn't always keep the law. So we are free from being slaves to the law. There is neither Jew nor Gentile, neither slave nor free, neither male and female – all are one in the Lord. Non-Jews were adopted into God's family; those who believe and obey Jesus are part of Abraham's ancestors and inherit the promises of God. Rigid views of the gospel pervert the truth and are a form of slavery.

Paul reminded his readers not to disregard the law or think that lawlessness was acceptable. Freedom from the law did not mean freedom to sin. Rather, Christians should be led by God's spirit and not commit immoral acts. Christians should love and serve one another with humility, for the entire law is summed up in one command: "Love your neighbor as yourself."

Stay away from acts such as sexual immorality, witchcraft and worshipping idols, hatred, arguing, jealousy, extreme anger, selfishness, and drunkenness. The fruit of the Spirit is love, joy, peace, patience, kindness, goodness, faithfulness, gentleness, and self-control. There is no law against these things. If someone is caught in a sin, restore the person gently. Help carry each other's burdens, don't compare your acts with the acts of others, and don't get tired of doing good to all people, especially other believers.

Letters to the Thessalonians

Paul wrote two letters to the church in Thessalonica, the large capital of Macedonia; Silas and Timothy were coauthors. Both letters were written soon after the three men were driven out of Corinth. The Thessalonica church was mainly composed of Gentiles, and Timothy had told Paul and Silas how well the church was doing.

In the first letter, the authors congratulated the believers on their conversion and growing faith. The church's faithfulness while being persecuted was a good example to the churches in other cities. Three important words – faith, love, and hope – appear early in the letter. Faith produced good works, love led to acts of kindness and mercy, and hope generated grit and endurance during difficult times. The authors also exhorted the believers with practical instructions about how to live.

> Avoid sexual immorality and conduct yourselves in a holy and honorable way. Lead a quiet life and mind your own business. Work so your life wins the respect of outsiders and so you won't have to depend on others. Live in peace with each other. Tell people not to be idle or disruptive, encourage those who are depressed, help the weak, and be patient with everyone. Make sure nobody does something wrong when they are mistreated, and always try to do what is good for each other and all others. Rejoice always, never stop praying, and give thanks in every situation.

The second, shorter letter was written soon after the first letter. The church was being persecuted, and some Christians believed it was a sign that Jesus would soon return to earth. False prophets reinforced this view because many Christians had been killed. Paul's first letter encouraged the believers to be watchful for Jesus and about the dead being raised, which added to their belief that Jesus's return could happen at any time. As a result, some believers had quit their jobs.

Paul explained that Jesus was not returning soon, and it might not happen for a long time. He explained that the time of Jesus's return is unknown, so people needed to go back to work. It was important for believers to work hard and not be a burden on others, just as the three men took care of their own needs. God would eventually punish wicked people.

Letters to the Corinthians

Paul wrote three letters to the believers in Corinth, but the first one was lost. In his second letter (known as First Corinthians), Paul responded to questions the church sent him. Corinth was a rough city with many taverns and people selling their bodies, and the church was struggling. Most of the believers were not well educated and were from a lower social class, so they felt inferior to others in the city. Paul told them that even though they were not wise by human standards, "God chose foolish things of the world to shame the wise and chose weak things of the world to shame the strong."

The people in the Corinth church had many practical questions. They asked how to deal with divisions and lawsuits within the church and with Christians who acted in immoral ways. They had questions about marriage, what foods could be eaten, and how to conduct useful worship services (such as celebrating the Lord's Supper, women in church, and exercising spiritual gifts). Church members also had questions about the resurrection of Jesus and their own resurrection in the future.

Paul pleaded to the church members to be unified rather than be divided based on who taught them. He also clarified what he had said about who Christians should be with and what kind of people to avoid.

> I planted the seed, Apollos watered it, but God made it grow. I laid a foundation and others build on it. If you fight about what teacher is best, it shows you are still babies in the faith. When you were babies in the faith, I gave you spiritual milk that you could handle. Your divisions show that you aren't ready for solid food.

> My previous letter said you shouldn't associate with people who committed improper sex acts. I didn't mean you should not associate with people of this world who are immoral, who lie and are greedy, or who worship other gods. If I meant that, you would have to leave the world! What I meant was that you must not associate with those *who claim to be your brother or sister in Christ* but who are doing these things. We are not to judge those outside the church – God will do that.

Paul explained that being guided by God's spirit was more important than having human wisdom. "If you have the Spirit, you have the mind of Christ." The human body was sacred and the temple of the Holy Spirit. Those who constantly committed major sins needed to be removed from the church and excluded from the Lord's Supper.

In regard to marriage, Paul said being single was good because it allowed people to serve God and others more freely. But because of our sexual nature, God blessed marriages because "it's better to be married than burn with uncontrolled passions." Those who get married need to give their bodies to each other, and neither party has power over the other. Paul also gave his opinions (not words from God) about other matters related to marriage and divorce.

Paul said a person can eat anything, but if a person thinks it's not right to eat something and then eats it, they have sinned. Eating becomes a stumbling block to those who have a less-developed faith. Therefore, Christians should not eat something if it causes another person to eat something they think they shouldn't eat. (Most of the meat eaten at the time had been sacrificed to idols.) Paul said, "I'm a Jew with Jews, but when I'm with others who don't follow rules about what to eat, I eat what they eat. I will be like others so they will be more willing to hear my message. God won't let you be tempted beyond what you can bear. When you are tempted, there is always a way to get out of it."

Paul wrote about how to conduct worship services. Believers needed to make sure they were sharing the Lord's Supper in peace. If people had disagreements with each other, they were to resolve it first. Paul said women should not talk or ask questions during worship if they didn't understand something – they should ask others about it later. Women were to avoid having disruptive side conversations and be quiet unless they were praying or teaching as part of the worship activities.

Paul said that too much time was being spent having people speak in other languages that nobody else understood. This was a gift given by the Spirit to some believers, but if nobody could interpret what was said, it wasn't useful, and others might think the church was full of people who were mentally ill. Everybody had a spiritual gift, such as healing, wisdom, knowledge, faith, understanding if a spirit is good, speaking another language, help, and guidance. Less-dramatic gifts given by the Spirit, such as preaching and understanding the truth about God, were more useful. Paul said, "I speak in tongues, but I'd rather speak five good words of instruction than speak 10,000 words in another language."

He spoke about the church as if it was a human body with many parts – everybody had a different function.

> The ear can't say, "Because I'm not an eye, I'm not part of the body." If the whole body were an eye, how could we hear? God created many parts of one body, and all the parts should work together. The parts that seem weaker are indispensable. If one part suffers, everybody suffers.

Paul then wrote that using spiritual gifts was not nearly as important as being a loving person.[4] Paul compared spiritual gifts and love this way:

> If I speak in another language but don't show love, I'm just making noise. If I have the gift of prophecy and can understand all mysteries, or if I have so much faith that I can move a mountain but I don't show love, I'm nothing. If I give everything I have to the poor and sacrifice my body but don't love others, I gain nothing.

> Love is patient and kind. It isn't jealous and doesn't brag or dishonor others. It's not proud or selfish. It doesn't get angry easily or keep track of when people do something wrong. Love doesn't delight in evil but rejoices with the truth. It bears and believes all things; it is always hopeful and endures all things. When I was a child, I talked and thought like a child. Now that I've matured, I've put away my childish and selfish ways. Love never fails. Faith, hope, and love are the most important, and the greatest of these is love.

---

[4] Paul used the Greek term *agape* as the word for love. The word involves action and sacrifice for others. It does not mean an emotional feeling, or friendship (*philia*), or physical love (*eros*).

Finally, Paul discussed the resurrection of the body, a strange concept to the Greeks. Everybody knew Jesus came back from the dead, and this meant others could come back from the dead. Jesus defeated death so a person's spiritual body will come back to life. Paul concluded with this mystery:

> When we are dead, we will be changed instantly when the last trumpet sounds. The dead will be raised and will live forever. What Hosea said will come true, "Death has been swallowed up in God's victory. Where, O death, is your victory; where is your sting?"

Paul's Last Letter to the Corinthians

Paul made several trips to Corinth to support and teach the believers, and some of his visits were "painful." Opposition to Paul had risen but the leader of a rebellion was disciplined. Paul expressed his joy that the church had dealt with this problem, and he encouraged the believers to allow the rebel leader back into the church. Since being a Christian in the Roman empire was hazardous, he reminded the church of the hope they had in the resurrection of their souls. They walked by faith and were new creatures because God lived in them – they had moved on from their old ways of acting and thinking. Believers are like pots of clay, shaped by the master potter, that perform different functions as God desires.

Paul spoke about all his qualifications to teach, but he also stressed his own weaknesses, including having a "thorn in the side." Paul never said anything about what bothered him, and he had prayed several times to have the problem removed. But God said "my power is shown in human weakness." Paul was good enough just as he was, and his limitations kept him humble – he was strong when he was weak.

Letter to the Romans

Paul's longest letter was sent to the house churches in Rome that had both Jewish and Gentile believers. He wrote before his first trip to Rome and didn't know many of the Christians in Rome personally, so his writing is more formal than the other letters he wrote.

His letter summarized the basic ideas of the Christian faith to believers who didn't have this knowledge. He explained the general principles of the faith systematically and logically, and his overall message was that Jesus died and delivered all people from sin, so a relationship with God is available to anybody who has faith in Jesus, the Christ. He used five themes to support this message:

- All people have a sinful nature.
- The death of Jesus was the best and last sacrifice of blood needed to take away the sins of the world and allow all people to be acceptable to God.
- Christians need to be holy and rely on God's Spirit to endure during difficult times. Deeper faith leads to deeper righteousness.
- Jews were initially chosen as God's people, but Gentiles are now included because the Israelites continually rejected God.
- Being a Christian means living in a different way in a sinful world.

People Have a Sinful Nature

The first theme was that individuals and society as a whole tend to do evil things. People commit all types of crimes and don't show mercy or fairness to others, even when they know there are consequences for doing so. They are proud and brag about how great they are and are not patient or kind. They hear the law but don't obey it, and they don't practice what they preach.

> Nobody is righteous, everybody has turned away from God. We can't be acceptable to God by obeying the law. Our inability to obey the law shows our sinful

nature. There is no difference between Jew and Gentile – all have sinned and fallen short of God's standards for righteousness.

Jesus, the Best and Last Sacrifice Needed

The second theme is that the death of Jesus was the best and last sacrifice of blood needed to take away the sins of the world and allows people to stand justified and righteous before God. The blood shed by Christ permanently stopped God's anger against people's sinful nature, just as the sacrifices of high-quality animals removed the sins of the Israelites. But those sacrifices only stopped God's anger temporarily. The sacrifice of Jesus is permanent and final and applies to everybody.

Abraham was "justified" (righteous) because of his faith. He obediently moved from Ur to Canaan and was ready to kill Isaac, even though God promised him countless descendants. He never lost hope for a son, even when he and Sarah were very old. He wasn't justified by obeying the law. A true Jew is somebody who is faithful to God's teachings, not somebody who has the outward characteristics of a Jew or obeys the law. "The sins of one man (Adam) affected all humans; the sacrifice of one man (Jesus) cleansed all humans."

The benefits of being a Christian are free because Jesus paid the price. People only need to have an earnest faith in Jesus to stand clean before God and gain the benefits. These benefits include having peace, joy, and hope, even during difficult times. Sin kills, but Jesus died to give us life.

Christian Holiness

A third theme focused on the processes of becoming mature in the Christian faith. People naturally do things they shouldn't do, but God's spirit helps them resist temptation and change their character. "All things work together for good for those who love God. Suffering produces perseverance, which produces character, which produces hope. If God is for us, who can be against us? Nothing can separate us from the love of Christ." Those who are guided by the Spirit aren't relying on their own resources. They are tapping into God's "living water," which gradually transforms them into people who reflect God's nature and character.

Updating the Promises to the Israelites

The fourth theme related to the issue of how Judaism relates to Christian beliefs. God chose the Israelites to be God's representatives on earth and Paul knew most Jews didn't believe Jesus was the Messiah. Jews expected the Messiah to be a king and overthrow the Romans. As a devout Pharisee, Paul fully understood the laws of Moses and had personal experience that allowed him to tie the ideas of Judaism with the new ideas of Christianity. The new promises are logically linked to the previous promises. A sovereign God could "elect" any group of people to be the chosen people. By focusing on obeying the law rather than having faith in God, the Jews lost their special status as God's chosen people. Now Gentiles who had faith in Jesus were included, adopted into God's family, a branch grafted onto a holy tree to replace dead branches. The Jews were still special to God, but when God included the Gentiles in the kingdom, there were more messengers who could bear fruit and carry the good news of God's saving love and forgiveness to all parts of the world. The Gentiles could also help the Jews understand God's overall plan for the world. God's love and mercy for the human race had not changed at all.

Living as Christians in the World

Paul ends by discussing what it took for a Christian to live in an evil world. Christians are to be obviously different.

> Don't conform to the ways and ideas of this world, but be changed by renewing your mind.
>
> Everybody should use their gifts to the best of their ability. Each person is part of one body, yet we all have

different functions and gifts. Some will preach while others will serve or teach; some will encourage or give generously while others will lead or show kindness.

Love must be sincere. Love one another and honor others more than yourself. Be happy in hope, patient during problems, and faithful in prayer. Share with other Christians who are in need and practice hospitality. Don't be proud and think of yourself more highly than you should. Instead, view yourself with realistic eyes.

Bless those who persecute you. Rejoice with those who rejoice; weep with those who weep. Do what you can to live at peace with everyone. Be willing to associate with people in low positions who do simple and dirty work. Hate what is evil, embrace what is good. Don't do evil to those who do evil to you, and do what everybody thinks is right. Don't seek revenge – that is something God will handle. Instead, "If your enemies are hungry, feed them; if they are thirsty, give them something to drink. In doing this, you will heap burning coals on their head."[5] Don't be overcome by evil, but overcome evil with good.

Submit to the government officials who provide justice. Give to those what you owe them: If you owe taxes or have debts, pay them. Respect and honor those who require it.

---

[5] This phrase has several meanings. It can be taken literally within the context of that culture, in which a person provides a large amount of charcoal to help a neighbor's dwindling fire. In ancient times, some people carried things on their heads. The phrase also has a deeper meaning — a person's extravagant generosity toward an enemy makes the enemy think about how they treat others. The result is to increase the chances of more peaceful relationships. The phrase does *not* mean hurting your enemy by burning their head in some way. The phrase is quoted because it appears in Proverbs.

Letter to the Colossians

The city of Colossae was 100 miles east of Ephesus and was on a major trade route connecting Asia and Europe. Paul had never been there, but he had visited cities near there and heard about its growing church composed mainly of Gentiles. Paul wrote to them to address false teachings that the church was facing that blended Jewish legalism, Greek philosophy, and Oriental mysticism.

The first half of the letter dealt with correct Christian doctrine. He stressed the supremacy of Jesus.

> Jesus is the visible image of the invisible God, the firstborn of all creation. All things on earth and in heaven, visible and invisible, were created by him and for him. He existed before all things, and he holds everything together. He is the head of the church and is supreme in everything. God's fullness lived in him, and through him all things on earth and in heaven are reconciled to God through the sacrifice of his blood on the cross.

Paul urged his readers to focus on Jesus rather than following strict Jewish practices, philosophies of angel worship, and ideas of self-denial. The blending of these additional elements into the faith took the people's attention away from the idea that Jesus was all Christians need to be right with God.

> Christ died so you don't need to follow the rules of this world that say, "Don't touch this, don't taste this!" These harsh rules are based on human teachings that appear to be wise but don't have any lasting value.

The second part of the letter discusses how Christians should behave, doing godly things and not evil things.

> Take off your old self and put on your new self. This means doing away with anger, saying lies about others, bad language, sexual immorality, evil desires, and selfishness. As God's chosen people, show compassion, kindness, humility, gentleness, and patience. Bear with each other and forgive one

another, just as Jesus forgives you. Most importantly, love others so you all stay together. Act wisely toward outsiders and make the most of every opportunity. Be patient and kind when talking to others.

Letter to the Ephesians

Paul wrote a longer and more sophisticated letter to the church in Ephesus that was similar to his letter to the Colossians. He sent both letters at about the same time while he was in prison in Rome. He had lived in Ephesus for several years, so he knew his audience well. There was no specific reason for writing other than to keep teaching the church what it meant to be the church.

While his letter to the Colossians stressed Jesus as the head of the church, his letter to the Ephesians focused on the church as the body of Christ, a collection of chosen people who were adopted into the faith. The general nature of the letter indicates that it was probably meant to be sent to the other churches in the region. Like the letter to the Colossians, his letter had two major parts – one on correct Christian ideas and the other about how to be faithful in the world.

The first part of the letter states that it was always part of God's larger plan to have all people on earth be in a loving relationship with God, not just the Jews. The three forms of God played a role in the development and continuation of God's overall plan. God the "Father" chose the believers; the Son (Jesus) made people holy through his death, which forgave all the sins of the world; and the Spirit guided people living on the earth. Paul stressed that people had done nothing to earn any special status with God. It was entirely God's grace, a free and undeserved gift that came to believers because of their faith in Jesus.

> You were previously dead in your sins, but now you are alive in Christ – your sins are forgiven. Grace has saved us because of our faith; it is God's free gift, not by what we have done so we can brag about it. We are God's handiwork and have been created to do good

works. God prepared us to do this long ago.

Jews and Gentiles are now one group with citizenship in heaven. God's purpose was to create one new humanity out of the two, thus making peace. Gentiles are no longer foreigners and strangers but fellow citizens with God's people and members of God's family which was built on the foundation of the apostles and prophets. Jesus is the chief cornerstone who holds the church together and rises to be God's holy temple.

Paul saw himself simply as God's servant to help reveal this overall plan to the Gentiles. He didn't want anybody feeling sorry for him while he was in prison—he was doing what he was meant to do.

These ideas were developed in the second part of the letter – instructions and encouragement for those in the church to live in peace with one another, despite their diversity, in order for the world to see an example of how people should live as one on the earth.

Showing unity within a diverse group had implications for individuals and the group. Each person had a different role, just as the different parts of the body help the entire body function. Paul wrote many of the same things he wrote to the Colossians about how Christians should live their lives and how to live in a community of faith. He expanded on his views about the roles within the family.

Submit to one another out of respect for Christ. Wives, submit yourselves to your husbands as you do to the Lord. Husbands, love your wives like Christ loved the church and gave himself up for her to make her holy. Love your wives as if they were your own body. He who loves his wife loves his own body, just as Jesus loves the church.

Children, obey your parents. Fathers, don't irritate your children; raise them with training and instruction about the Lord. Slaves, obey your masters with respect and sincerity. Masters, treat your slaves in the same way. Don't threaten them, for our Master in heaven shows no favoritism. Serve others as if you were serving the Lord, who will reward us based on what we do, not whether we are a slave or free.

Paul ended his letter by encouraging the church to be on guard against evil while being strong to keep and expand the faith. "Our struggle is not against flesh and blood, but against the powers of darkness in this world and against the spiritual forces of evil." Using the analogy of a soldier's armor, he described defensive and offensive tools to fight the devil.

Letter to the Philippians

Philippi was a prosperous Roman city in Macedonia, and the Gentiles in the church were Roman citizens who supported Paul financially. He wrote his letter from prison in Rome and is very personal. He gave an update on his travels and thanked them for their financial support. He talked about how being in prison helped spread the gospel – the guards and Roman officials were hearing the good news about Jesus.

Paul encouraged the Philippians to stand firm in their faith and rejoice when they were persecuted for their faith. He wasn't worried about dying – he would gain from it by being even closer to God. He wrote about the importance of being humble and used Jesus as the ultimate example of humility, which was not considered a virtue among the people who lived at that time.

> Be of one mind and don't do anything out of selfish ambition. Be humble and value others and their interests above your own. In your relationships with others, have the same attitude that Jesus had. Even though he was a form of God, he didn't consider equality with God as something he should use to his advantage. Instead, he became a human servant and obeyed God, dying in a humiliating way on a cross. As a result, God honored him to be in the highest place and gave him the highest name. Everything in heaven, on earth, and under the earth will bow down to him, and everyone will say that Jesus Christ is Lord.

Paul talked about his own credentials as a devout Jew. He could have boasted about his religious background and holiness, but these were irrelevant—he gave up his privileges in the religious community to believe in Jesus and promote the good news. He was still learning and trying to understand Jesus more, even if it meant dying for his faith.

> Don't be anxious about anything. In every situation, present your requests to God by praying with thanks. The peace of God which is beyond our understanding will guard your hearts and minds. Whatever is true, noble, right, and pure, think about these things. I've learned to be at peace in every situation. I know what it's like to be in need and to have plenty, to be hungry or well fed. I can do all things through Christ who gives me strength and what I need.

Paul said a Christian's citizenship is in heaven and believers are ambassadors for the kingdom of God to those living on earth. Christianity represented a new model of thinking and living, and the Spirit transforms and protects believers on their mission in this world.

Letters to Church Leaders

Paul wrote letters during and after he was in prison in Rome to pastors who lived in areas he had visited. The letters focused mainly on organizing the leadership of the church, teachings about good conduct in the world, and dealing with false teachings.

Titus

Titus was a Greek Gentile who became a believer during Paul's first trip to Asia Minor and was with Paul and Barnabas when they went to Jerusalem to tell the church leaders about the conversion of the Gentiles. He was used as an example during the discussion about the need for circumcision among the Gentiles, and he eventually became the leader of all the churches on the island of Crete.

Paul told Titus to appoint leaders ("elders") for the churches on the island. Elders were to show the fruits of the spirit (e.g., being patient, kind, hospitable, self-controlled, disciplined). They needed to be strong believers: acting with holiness, holding firmly to the Christian message, encouraging others with correct teaching and opposing those who didn't believe it, being faithful to their wives, and not being violent or drinking too much alcohol. In fact, these qualities should be exhibited by all believers, regardless of their position or gender. This would help people respect and admire those who followed Jesus.

Paul told Titus to crack down on the Jews who were saying bad things about Gentile believers who were not following the Jewish customs. He also told Titus to teach all believers not to rebel against the government leaders, to do good whenever they could, and to avoid talking about foolish and useless controversies. Those who caused divisions should be warned several times, and if they continued being divisive, they should be avoided.

Philemon

Paul's shortest letter (one page) was written while he was a prisoner in Rome. He met and converted a slave named Onesimus (meaning "useful") while they were both in prison. The slave belonged to Philemon, a Christian living in Colossae who led a house church. Paul had helped Philemon become a believer. Onesimus had taken some of Philemon's money and run away to Rome and was being released from prison. Paul convinced him to return to Philemon and be useful rather than be useless like a missing slave. Paul's letter encouraged Philemon to take in Onesimus again and treat him as a fellow believer and not punish or kill him as he would do to a typical runaway slave. Paul promised to pay Philemon the money he was owed by Onesimus. (Onesimus was freed by Philemon and went on to become the bishop of the church in Ephesus; Philemon became the bishop of the church in Gaza. Both men were eventually killed by the Romans because of their faith.)

Timothy

Paul wrote two letters to Timothy, the half-Gentile Christian who was his traveling companion. Although Timothy was young, Paul left him in charge of leading the large and diverse church in Ephesus because of his preaching and teaching skills.

In his first letter, Paul warned Timothy about Jews who were teaching incorrect ideas about what was required to be a Christian. Their emphasis was on obeying the laws of Moses, not loving others and having faith in Jesus. The law was still useful when it dealt with criminals, liars, rebels, slave traders, and those who practiced sexual immorality.

Paul also wrote about how to organize worship services and the church. He gave instructions about how to pray, how women should dress, and who should speak and teach during worship. He gave Timothy many of the same instructions he gave Titus about the qualifications for the elders (also called bishops), and he discussed the qualifications of the deacons.

He gave Timothy advice about how to maintain his health and noted that paying elders for their work was a good idea. Paul encouraged him to pursue godliness and show faith, love, endurance, and gentleness to others. Finally, Paul gave him advice about how to deal with believers in every part of life: those who were old and young, married or widowed or single, slaves and their masters, those who were accused of a sin, and the rich and poor.

> Be content with what you have. Those who want to get rich fall into a trap. Many foolish desires are harmful and ruin people, for the love of money causes all kinds of evil. Some who are eager for money have left the faith and have had many problems. Those who are rich in this life shouldn't be proud or put their hope in their possessions that can be uncertain. They should put their hope in God who richly provides everything we need to be happy. Tell people to do good and be rich in good deeds, being generous and willing to share.

Paul's second letter was written much later when he was suffering in a cold prison cell in Rome because he was a Christian. Paul believed he would soon be killed by the Romans under Nero, and it was the last record of any of his writings. All Christians were being persecuted at the time and many of his friends abandoned him, so he was feeling alone.

Although Paul was depressed, he encouraged Timothy to keep the faith and not be afraid of dying because of his faith. Suffering was part of the Christian life, and dying meant being closer to God. Paul warned Timothy about false teachers who spent time quarreling about things that were not important. Those who opposed him should be dealt with gently so they would come to their senses and turn back to the truth.

Paul also told Timothy to continue preaching and teaching from the scriptures, which had made him wise and understand the words and thoughts of God. The scriptures were all useful for teaching, correcting, and training others in holy living. The inspired scriptures help equip Christians for every good work.

Paul ended his last letter by asking Timothy to visit him in prison. Luke was the only person left in Rome who comforted and encouraged him. (There is nothing written about whether Timothy arrived in Rome before Paul was executed.)

16
OTHER LETTERS TO BELIEVERS

Paul wrote most of the letters in the Bible, but other letters were written by the apostles Peter and John and the two half-brothers of Jesus, James and Judas (called Jude). Another letter was written by an unknown author to Jews in general. This chapter summarizes these letters.

Peter's Letters

Peter wrote two letters to believers. The first letter was sent to Gentile believers in cities Paul visited who were being attacked verbally and physically for their faith. The letter was sent to encourage believers to remain strong in their faith as they suffered in difficult times, just as Jesus did. Believers should love one another, be good citizens, and have good families in order to give a good impression to others. In the end, they would be rewarded in heaven.

> God is pleased when you suffer and endure for doing good. You are a chosen people, a holy nation, and God's special possession so you may speak about Jesus who called you out of darkness into his light. Your beauty should not come from what you wear – it should be your inner self, the unfading beauty of a gentle and quiet spirit. Be prepared to answer everyone who asks you why you have hope, but do it with respect and gentleness. Above all, love each other deeply, for love covers many sins. Be alert and sober because your enemy, the devil, prowls like a roaring lion looking for somebody to devour. Resist him and

stand firm in the faith – the family of believers all over
the world is experiencing the same kind of suffering.

Peter's second letter is shorter and focused on resisting
false teachers and evildoers who influenced the church. The
diversity of the early church brought with it new ideas that
were not consistent with the teachings of Christian leaders,
and Peter wanted to emphasize the church's basic teachings.

He told believers to grow in their faith. "Make every
effort to add to your faith the qualities of goodness,
knowledge, self-control, perseverance, godliness, support
for others, and love. These qualities will help you be effective
and productive." He wrote that true prophets always speak
for God and from God and don't rely on their own ideas to
influence others; false teachers tell stories to take advantage
of gullible believers.

One of the false teachings was that Jesus would not
return and there would be no final judgment. Peter stressed
that Jesus would return and be the final judge. Evil would be
destroyed with fire, just as evil was destroyed by water in the
days of Noah. The day was unknown because "a day is like
a thousand years" to God, and eventually the false teachers
would be judged harshly.

Letter from James

James was a half-brother of Jesus and did not follow Jesus
initially, but he became a believer after the resurrection.
James led the Jerusalem church that Paul addressed when
discussing issues related to the Gentiles. His letter was
addressed to Jews living outside of Palestine and focused
on what it means to follow Jesus.

The letter is basically a manual for correct Christian
conduct, so it assumes those who read it were well-
informed Jews who were now Christians. The book rambles
in different directions and discusses different topics.

> Be glad when you face trials, for tests of your faith
> produce perseverance, which leads to maturity. Those
> who persevere receive a crown of life .... If you lack

wisdom, ask God for it and you will receive it …. If you are tempted, it's because you have evil desires. These desires give birth to sin. God doesn't do the tempting; only good things come from above. It's in God's unchanging nature to do good and not do evil …. Don't just listen to God's words – do what is said …. Those who consider themselves religious but don't control their tongue have a worthless religion …. A person with a pure religion takes care of orphans and widows in their distress and isn't polluted by the ways of this world …. Don't favor the rich and those who look nice. Love everybody equally. The wealth of the rich will be destroyed because of their self-indulgence …. Don't put too much faith in your own plans. You don't know what will happen in the future. It might happen if God wants it to happen …. Confess your sins to each other and pray for each other so that you may be healed. Prayers of righteous people are powerful.

James's other main message comes in his attack on those who see a difference between people who claim to have faith and those who do good deeds. The two go together: "A person's faith is dead if it is not accompanied by action. The faith of our ancestors was always shown by what they did."

Letters from Jude and John

Jude was the brother of James and the half-brother of Jesus. Like Peter's first letter, Jude focused on addressing false teachings that were spreading in the church. There is nothing written in this very short book (less than one page long) about his audience and the false teachings. Jude simply speaks strongly against the false teachers who misrepresent the concept of grace and the role of Jesus. These teachers were highly critical of things they didn't understand. Jude listed many examples of God's judgment and said false teachers would be punished one day, just as God punished the false prophets and teachers who lived among the Jews.

Letters from John

John was the fisherman who became one of the original 12 disciples. He wrote a long account about the life of Jesus, and he wrote three general letters to Christians late in the first century AD.

His first letter aimed to encourage and strengthen the church that faced false teachings. The heresy of Gnosticism was developing that thought all physical things are evil and only the spirit is good. This meant that it was the spirit of Jesus that counted, not his body; some believed Jesus was not even human. This belief led Gnostics to live immoral lives because keeping the law had no consequences. The Gnostics were very proud of their beliefs and looked down on those who didn't believe the way they did.

John opposes each of the Gnostic views. He was a close personal friend and experienced the reality of Jesus's physical life; Jesus was God in physical form. John also stressed righteous living, humility, and loving others. A true Christian believes Jesus was the Messiah and the Son of God, obeys Jesus's commands, lives a good life, and loves other Christians.

> This is what love is: Jesus died for us. We should be willing to die for other Christians. If anyone has material possessions and sees Christians in need but doesn't help them, how can the love of God be in the person? Let us love with our actions. Let us love one another, for love comes from God. Everyone who loves has been born of God. Those who do not love do not know God, because God is love. There is no fear in love. Perfect love drives out fear because fear relates to punishment. We love because Jesus first loved us. Jesus gave this command: Anyone who loves God must also love their brother and sister.

John's second letter was very short and warned the church about false teachers who influenced the church without its knowledge. John said the church should have nothing to do with such people. John repeated the two points he made in his first letter: the need for members of the church to obey Jesus's commands and to love each other.

John's third letter was also short and was sent to instruct a friend about how to handle an unusual situation in the church. A teacher who John had sent to support various churches was not accepted by the leader of one of the churches. This leader acted like a bully, controlled people, and even expelled some believers who helped other visiting teachers. John thanked his friend for helping the teachers who had visited, and he indirectly warned the leader that he would soon deal with him in person.

Letter to the Hebrews

Hebrews was written to Jews to convince them that Jesus was superior to all the other heroes of the Old Testament. It was meant to keep Jewish believers from going back to Judaism. Although Hebrews is called a letter, it's structured like an essay. It begins by discussing how God spoke first through the prophets but now spoke through Jesus.

> God spoke previously to our ancestors through the prophets at many times and in various ways, but in these last days, God has spoken to us through Jesus. He was appointed the heir of all things, and God used him to make the universe. Jesus is the exact representation of God and his words hold the world together. Now that he purified us from our sins, he sits at the right hand of God in heaven. He is far superior to any angel in heaven.

The author frequently refers to Jesus as being "better than" the heroes of the Old Testament. The author explains how Christ is better than the angels, better than Abraham and Moses, better than Joshua and all the priests. The New Covenant – Jesus's sacrifice that cleansed people of their sins and provides everlasting life to all of God's people, the church – is better than the Old Covenant. Jesus's sacrifice is better than the sacrifices performed under the Old Covenant, and experiencing Jesus is better than experiencing the events on Mount Sinai. Jesus is the great high priest who intercedes for the people to God and is also the Judge.

> The word of God is alive and sharper than any double-edged sword. It judges our hidden thoughts – nothing is hidden from God's sight. Everything is opened and laid bare before God to whom we must give account. We have a high priest who can empathize with our weaknesses. Jesus was tempted in every way, just as we are, but he did not sin.

Jesus came into the world as the ultimate sacrifice. It was impossible for the blood of bulls and goats to take away sins. Sacrifices to eliminate the stain of sin were no longer needed. But the deliverance from sin did not give people permission to use that freedom to keep sinning. Instead, a Christian's focus should be to "encourage one another to show our love and good deeds." Those who have faith in Jesus should be bold and persevere through difficult times and not be timid.

> Faith is the certainty of things we hope for and confidence in what we have not seen. Our faith helps us believe what God has done. It was Abraham's faith that led him to leave his home in Ur and move to Canaan and to know he and Sarah would have a child at an old age. We had faith in God when Moses led us through the waters to escape the Egyptians. Nearly everybody died before seeing the promised land, but they could see it from a distance and did not doubt because they had faith in God's promises to us.
>
> By faith the walls of Jericho fell, and by faith the prostitute Rahab was not killed because she welcomed the spies. I don't have time to talk about Gideon, Barak, Samson, Jephthah, David, Samuel, and the prophets. Through faith they conquered kingdoms, provided justice, and gained what was promised. They shut the mouths of lions, quenched the fury of the flames, and escaped the edge of the sword. Their weakness turned into strength as they became powerful in battle.

Others were tortured and faced jeers, beatings, and imprisonment. They were put to death by stoning, sawed in two, and killed with a sword. They wore the skins of sheep and goats and were poor and homeless, persecuted, and mistreated. They wandered in deserts and mountains, living in caves and holes in the ground.

Since we are surrounded by such a great cloud of witnesses, get rid of everything that stops us and the sin that traps us. Strengthen your feeble arms and weak knees and run the race we face with perseverance. Fix your eyes on Jesus who endured the cross and now sits next to God's throne.

The author ends by telling the Jews to keep living a moral and loving life, showing hospitality to strangers, and remembering those who were in prison and who suffered because they were mistreated.

17
STRANGE MESSAGES FORESEE A CATACLYSMIC FINALE

Jesus talked about the kingdom of God as if it already existed on earth but also that it was still coming. He said a king would judge people like a shepherd separates sheep from goats, sending sheep to heaven and goats to hell. Jesus spoke privately to his disciples when they asked him about the events at "the end of the age." Jesus told them:

> You will hear about wars and rumors of wars, famines, and earthquakes, but these are just birth pangs. There will be tribulations and many will hate you because you follow me. Many will fall away and betray others, and false prophets will lead many astray. The end will come after the gospel is preached to all nations. When you see the Antichrist standing in the Temple, as Daniel predicted, you need to flee as fast as you can. The persecution will be like no other, and if time was not cut short, nobody would survive. False prophets will tell you Jesus has returned and the end is coming, but don't believe them, for these things must happen first.

The Christians thought Jesus would return soon as a king to save them from abuse and persecution. Their hope was not that they would avoid terrible times but that they would soon be with Jesus. He told parables about being ready for his return.

But by the end of the first century AD, it was clear Jesus was not returning anytime soon. The Romans had destroyed Jerusalem and the Temple, and according to the predictions about the return of the Messiah, both needed to exist. Nobody knew when the predictions about when he would return, eliminate evil, and judge all who lived in the world would occur. During his ministry, Jesus told a parable about the coexistence of good and bad.

> The kingdom of heaven is like what happened to a farmer who sowed good seeds of wheat in his field. While everybody slept, his enemy planted weed seeds in the field and left quietly. When the wheat sprouted, the weeds also appeared. The farmer's workers asked him, "Didn't you sow good seed in your field? Where did the weeds come from?"
>
> The farmer replied, "An enemy did this."
>
> The servants asked the man, "Should we pull up the weeds?"
>
> The farmer said, "No, if you pull up the weeds, you will also uproot some of the wheat. Let both of them grow together until the harvest. Then I will tell the harvesters to collect the weeds and tie them in bundles to be burned. Then they will gather the wheat and bring it to my barn."

So Jesus may not return for a very long time. Meanwhile, believers live alongside those who are not believers and will live on earth with their citizenship in heaven. Churches are like small colonies that show the rest of the world a bit of what heaven will look like. The kingdom of God has come in part but will be complete when Jesus returns and evil is destroyed.

Many predictions have come true about the Israelites and the Messiah, but there are still a few predictions about what will happen in the future that have not yet happened. These predictions mainly relate to the "end of time" return of the Messiah and the separation of people going to either heaven or hell. Some of the predictions are highly symbolic and full with vivid images, and the prophets who received them from God did not know what they meant. Because of the ongoing persecution, Christians were interested in any details they could get about when their pain might end. They endured with hope rather than feeling sorry for themselves.

Near the end of the first century, John, the fisherman who was one of the first disciples, was a pastor in Ephesus. He resisted the Romans that wanted to kill Christians because they did not pledge allegiance to the emperor and worship him (Daniel faced this situation when he did not worship King Nebuchadnezzar). Ultimately, the Romans sent John to live alone on the Greek island of Patmos.

Difficulty Understanding Apocalyptic Literature

When John was on Patmos, he wrote the book of Revelation using a popular type of literature at that time that related to the destruction of the world (the apocalypse). Apocalyptic literature used highly symbolic language, such as strange animals and special numbers, and usually lacked important details. The content was hard to understand and could mean many different things. This type of literature was used by a few Old Testament prophets and New Testament authors.

Christians were being persecuted for not obeying Roman laws that violated the principles of their faith.[6] John wanted to communicate with members of the church from a distance, but it was dangerous for him to be clear in his letters. Since the lives of those receiving the letter could be in danger if the letter was read by Roman officials, John used terms that had double meanings or would only be understood by believers. It was similar to how an athletic team or members of an underground community use secret signs and terms to communicate with each other: his words were in code and were not to be taken literally. For example, he talked about the evils of Babylon, but he was really talking about the evils of the Roman empire. He often used

---

[6] In the last decade of the first century, the Roman emperor Domitian severely persecuted the Christians and gave himself the title "Lord and God" and wanted everybody to worship him.

the number seven to symbolize completeness (seven cities and hills, seven seals, seven stars, seven trumpets).

Encouragement to Seven Churches

The first three chapters of Revelation were directed to seven churches in Asia Minor, starting with Ephesus. The cities were connected by a major road, and the letter was meant to be sent to the next church along a circular route.

Persecution had caused believers in each city to compromise their beliefs and actions in order to blend in with nonbelievers. John wrote to encourage them to resist the temptation to worship the Roman emperor and stay true to their beliefs. Believers should have hope because God is in charge and will eventually win the war against evil.

John adjusted his messages to the specific situation that each local church faced. For example, Laodicea was a prosperous city, and the people in its church were lazy and self-sufficient. Although the city was a center for banking, John said the church was spiritually poor; although the city produced beautiful clothes, John said the believers were naked; although the city had a medical school, he said the church was blind. The hot springs in the area were good for bathing, and cold water was refreshing in the heat. The hot water that flowed to the city via aqueducts turned lukewarm by the time it reached them, and lukewarm water was used to cause vomiting. John told those in the church these words from God:

> I know you are neither cold nor hot. Because you are lukewarm, I'm about to spit you out of my mouth! You say, "I am rich, I have acquired wealth and don't need anything." But you don't realize you are poor, blind, and naked. I rebuke and discipline those I love.

But despite the church's laziness and pride, John reminded the church of God's goodness. God says, "I stand at your door and knock. If you hear my voice and open the door, I will come in and be with you." The choice is always there for an individual to respond, without being forced, to the invitation to know God. A central theme of the scriptures is that after sin and judgment, God provides love and grace rather than punishment.

The End of History

After writing to the seven churches, John wrote about visions of the future that came from God as a message to all believers. He described a set of events associated with the end of time when Jesus will return from heaven. There will be "birth pangs" that signal the final events are coming, and then the final events will occur.

John described the final events of history in terms of a "tribulation" (years of intense persecution of Christians, accompanied by many natural disasters and warfare), a "beast" (an evil power that uses its powers against the Christians), the Antichrist (a false prophet identified by the number 666),[7] a final battle between the forces of good and evil at Armageddon (a valley in northern Israel), a "millennium" (1,000 years of peace), and the return of Christ who defeats all the powers of darkness and burns all evil. God's kingdom will then be established in heaven and on earth without any evil being present. The idea of a "rapture" is based on other Biblical passages and doesn't appear in John's revelation. This event is when Jesus comes again and Christians rise into the sky to accompany him back to earth.

It's not clear how all these characters and events work together. Some people believe that the rapture will come first, then the tribulation, followed by the second coming of Christ and the millennium. Then a final rush of evil occurs,

---

[7] The meaning of 666 is unknown. Attempts have been made to identify the person using a numbering system associated with the alphabet. Many scholars think it symbolized incompleteness (the number 7 symbolized completeness, so 666 was not quite 777), and it may refer to a Roman emperor. The Dutch thought it related to the year when they lost a major naval battle in 1666. Many claimed Adolf Hitler met the conditions of the Antichrist.

after which Christ comes back a third time and defeats evil in one final battle. Others believe that Christians will experience the rapture *after* the tribulation; after that comes the millennium, followed by the return of Christ and the final judgment. Another view is that we are already in the millennium and the tribulation will come before the rapture.

There is a rationale for each view, and other combinations are possible. But because of the mysteries of the symbolism and the lack of details about how and when the events will happen, nobody really knows how all these events will unfold. Many scholars believe the events apply in a general sense and can be interpreted within the context of events at multiple times of history, with the key point that Christians should persevere and have hope during times of extreme hardship. In this perspective, the revelations are not meant to predict specific events in the future. For many believers, it's enough to know there is a happy ending despite a painful process.

A sign that the end of time is approaching is the construction of the Temple for the third time in Jerusalem. The Antichrist is predicted to serve in the Temple, only to turn on the Jews and persecute them. Many natural disasters, such as earthquakes, famine, and darkened skies, are predicted to occur in the final days.[8] John repeated some details that Isaiah and Paul said would happen about the return of Jesus: those who have died will come back to life again as Jesus did, and every creature, dead or alive, will bow and honor Jesus as the King and Lord of the universe.

A number of awful things are predicted to take place before a final battle between good and evil takes place. The good forces are led by a shining king, the "Lion of Judah, the Root of David" (Jesus), who is "worthy to receive

---

[8] The creation of the nation of Israel in 1948 after nearly 1,900 years without a national status has prompted some Christians and Jews to believe it is a sign that the end of time is coming soon. More severe natural disasters and changes in the world's climate support their beliefs.

power, wealth, wisdom, strength, honor, glory, and praise." Various natural disasters, plagues, wars, and terror will be carried out by evil men.

Evil will grow so strong and widespread in hell's all-out desperate attempt to defeat the forces of good that God will have seen enough, and it will be time for the judgment. A battle among many nations will take place, and the description of the battle closely resembles modern-day warfare – the sounds of thunderous jets, bombs and missiles falling from the sky, flashes of light and rumbling earth, and widespread destruction. Evil forces attack heaven but are defeated by God's army of angels, led by the archangel Michael. Babylon is destroyed because of its immorality, false religions, and the comforts of materialism. Individuals are then judged, and nonbelievers will be crushed like grapes in a winepress. God then throws most of the evil powers into a lake of fire.

Evil still exists but has no influence on the earth, which leads to a long period of peace. This shows people what life can be like without the influence of evil. Later, Satan will be unleashed and evil forces will surround the people of God, but Satan and all remaining forces of evil will be thrown into a lake of fire where they will be continually tormented for eternity – they will finally get what they deserve.

A New Heaven and a New Earth

Those in heaven will rejoice at the destruction of evil and sing, "Hallelujah, for the Lord God Almighty reigns." The holy city of Jerusalem will be restored on earth, and God's dwelling place (heaven) will be among the people. The king on his throne says:

> There will be no more tears in their eyes and no more death or crying or pain. The old things have passed away and I have made everything new! It is done. I am the Alpha and the Omega, the Beginning and the End. To the thirsty I will give free water from the spring of the water of life. The victors will inherit all this. I will be their God, and they will be my children.

The foundation and walls of the holy city are spectacular. There is no sun or moon because the glory of God always provides light, and there is no darkness. Those whose names are in the book of life will live as the bride of God forever. Like in the book of Job, the pain and suffering of God's people end, and the perseverance of the faithful results in a happy ending. Spiritual battles end and there is total victory as evil is destroyed forever.

John ends by writing that it was Jesus who told him to write about his vision to the church. Jesus says to all, "I'm coming soon. Let those who are thirsty come to me." Amen.

EPILOGUE

Revelation was the last book written by an eyewitness of Jesus's life that was included in the Bible. The Christian movement grew rapidly throughout the Roman Empire thanks in part to the 200 years of peace in the empire and an excellent road system. These made it easier for people to travel safely over long distances. The Jews were scattered throughout the empire after Jerusalem was destroyed in AD 70, and they took with them an understanding of the God of Abraham and the history of the Israelites and its prophets. This made the messages of those spreading news about Jesus more understandable.

Although Christianity was an illegal religion and many believers were killed throughout the empire, an account written in about AD 200 said Christians "filled the cities, islands, fortresses, towns, marketplaces, the army itself, tribes, companies, the Imperial Palace, the Senate, the Forum." In other words, Christians were everywhere.

Justin Martyr tried to convince the Roman government that Christians were good citizens, even though they would not worship the Roman gods, but he was killed with some of his disciples in AD 165. Other Christian leaders were persecuted and killed in gruesome ways. Because of the strong persecution against the Christians, most believers at that time thought they were in the midst of the tribulation. The Roman Empire eventually stopped persecuting Christians in AD 313 during Constantine's rule, but more than 1,700 years later, Christians are still persecuted in some parts of the world.

In 1517, a monk in Germany named Martin Luther raised concerns about the religious practices and ideas of the Roman Catholic Church. His protests led to the Protestant movement, and other religious scholars started new forms of the church. Since that time, many other Protestant groups ("denominations") have formed based on their different religious views. The power of the church was reduced as each believer's interpretation of the scriptures became more acceptable. If people did not like what was being taught or anything else that happened in their church, they simply went elsewhere or did not continue being part of any church. Meanwhile, the Catholic Church has been led by one person (the Pope) and has stayed intact while it changes some of its traditions over time.

In the past 200 years, there has been more interest by some groups of Christians to spread the news about Jesus throughout the world, often as they provide services to others, such as education and medical care. Jesus's final words on earth commanded believers to "make disciples of all the nations" (the "Great Commission" found in Matthew 28:19–20). The word *nation* applies to different types of people, not governments, and this command has motivated some Christians to find groups of people in remote areas of the world who have not yet heard the stories about Jesus and communicate these stories to them in terms they will understand.

In the early 1800s, a preacher named Charles Finney started a revival movement to get people to return to the church and to convert people to Christianity. He used different methods to increase the number of converts, and a new way to define a successful Christian and church related to the number of people who decide to follow Jesus.

In the past 150 years, Protestant churches in the United States have differed significantly in their approach to various social issues, such as slavery and racial relations, and religious issues, such as the truthfulness of the scriptures and how important it is to care for people's physical needs. These differences have led to many divisions within the church. The label *Christian* now means many different things.

Those who call themselves Christian represent about 30% of the world's population, making Christianity the world's largest religious group. About half of the 2.4 billion Christians are Catholic, and most Christians are found in Africa, Asia, and Latin America. Muslims represent the second largest religious group (about 25% of the world population), and Islam has the fastest growth rate among the world's major religions.

AUTHOR'S PERSPECTIVE

The early chapters of the Bible describe God's beautiful creation that was damaged by evil forces. People were given the ability to tell the difference between right and wrong and the freedom to choose their own way to live. Those who are selfish and do not follow God eventually harm themselves and others. God always forgives and loves all people even though nobody is perfect. God's support for people often helps those who do not believe, while at the same time, evil in the world affects those who follow God. Life is not fair and we often don't know what will happen in our lives.

Evil Forces Still Exist

The predictions made in Revelation about the destruction of evil have obviously not yet come true. Many bad things in the world still cause pain, suffering, and death. Evil forces quietly affect many aspects of life and try to disrupt the forces of good in individuals and in society. Meanness and unfairness are still signs of evil influences in the world.

Paul told those in Ephesus, "Our struggle is against the rulers and authorities and the spiritual forces of evil" (Ephesians 6:12). The ways of evil can be attractive – Satan poses as "an angel of light" and influences people to follow the wrong path. The end result of evil action is often some form of terrible pain, and nobody knows when the evil in this world will end.

Those who follow and practice the teachings of Jesus represent the kingdom of heaven to others on earth. Just as today's ambassadors to other countries do not obey laws that violate the laws and requirements of their home country, Christians are to live in this world but not violate God's requirements. Individually and as a group, Christians are to be examples of God's love and forgiveness. God's people, the church, are to have a different way of thinking and acting. Christians are God's "exhibit A" to the world about how people should live on earth and promote peace in the midst of conflict.

Being God's Ambassador Is Very Challenging

Being an effective ambassador is not an easy task. Christians are not perfect examples, and the church is constantly being attacked by evil forces that try to minimize the efforts of believers and the organizations they create. One strategy used by evil forces is to reduce the influence and messages of the church by creating divisions, distractions, and doubts and by making minor things important while more important things are ignored. As a result, Christians often talk about religious ideas but do not act with love.

Another way evil affects the church is by slowly influencing Christians to embrace the local culture. Paul warned Christians about letting the world "squeeze you slowly into its own mold" and told Christians to "be changed by constantly renewing your mind" (Romans 12:2). The world thinks success is defined by a person's wealth, health, and comfortable life. By this definition, many Christians are successful, yet none of these provide lasting happiness or inner joy, and none are valid measures of spiritual success.

Relatively few believers make a significant difference in the world because this requires following God's priorities. Making a difference requires self-sacrifice, sometimes to the point of death. We must all decide what to do with our lives, what to live for and what to die for. Following Jesus requires people to make sacrifices and help others.

Jesus's parable of the farmer who sowed described in chapter 10 discusses this challenge. Two of the three types of seeds that take root produce no crop. One type refers to those who fall away when things get hard because they are not yet mature in their faith. The other type refers to those who are choked by life's worries, riches, and pleasures. Making a difference in the world is challenging!

Christians are called to fight the forces of evil with love and compassion and to promote fairness for all people.

God requires people to "act fairly, love kindness, and walk humbly with God" (Micah 6:8). Jesus condemned the Pharisees for making their religion a show but not doing these three things. In fact, Jesus only got angry when he spoke to religious leaders who said one thing but did another, who judged others harshly, and who used religion to further their own interests.

Micah's message is simple, but living it is very hard. It is only possible through the slow and steady process of becoming more like Jesus and by being led by God's spirit to act in ways that provide healing and hope to others. The task is easier when others support those who do these things. The kingdom of God on earth grew rapidly because the early Christians loved others in unusual ways. They were the sheep who fed the hungry, gave a drink to the thirsty, invited the stranger in, clothed the naked, cared for the sick, and visited those in prison. True faith and belief are shown through one's actions, not by what a person says.

Christians who reflect God's character exhibit certain types of "fruit." Paul told the early believers, "The fruit of the Spirit is love, joy, peace, patience, kindness, goodness, faithfulness, gentleness, and self-control" (Galatians 5:22–23). Those who call themselves Christians but do not exhibit these fruits are not good models to follow. We will know mature Christians by their love for others, not by what they say they believe.

Is It Worth It?

I have found deep happiness and meaning by studying the events and teachings of the Bible and pursuing a life that serves others. My beliefs are demonstrated through my actions, and the experiences of my life and others have convinced me that God is very real and Jesus is the best example to follow.

My life has unfolded in unplanned ways and has been an incredible adventure. I stayed open to all possibilities, and like Abraham when he was called by God while living in Ur, I have listened and acted without knowing where I was going. I haven't been afraid to take risks, and I want my life to have meaning. I now look back and see how and why God closed doors I was pursuing while opening others that were more compatible with God's plans. God's invisible hand has blessed me all my life. I have experienced normal human sufferings but have also been spared from extreme hardships and temptations. When I experienced miracles, they came at just the right moment. They convinced me God is always present, so I don't need to worry.

I don't need hard scientific proof of God's existence to believe or act, for "not everything that counts can be counted" (a quote attributed to Albert Einstein). There is an overwhelming amount of evidence of God's presence in the world. I and many others have experienced things that have no logical explanation.

My faith and experiences give me hope for the future and the inspiration and energy to love others without expecting anything in return. The longer I live, the more I'm convinced that love and service are what the world needs now more than ever, even if there is no reward after death. Jesus is a trustworthy but unseen guiding light. He used his power for the good of others, not for himself. Those who study and follow his example of love, service, forgiveness, humility, and grace while living in a violent world will make today's world a better place.

A life of service may be exhausting and dangerous, but it does not have to lead to burnout. The branches of a tree don't struggle to make fruit – they simply stay connected to the living tree. When a person is thirsty for fresh water in a dry desert, they find a well and crank the handle of a pump over and over again until water comes out. As long as the pump's line extends deep into fresh water, using the pump produces water easily. The pump is an instrument to bless those in need, and it continues to function regardless of how many times it is cranked. The secret to staying fresh for constant service is staying connected to the living source of water that sustains life.

The Christian life can be risky. Speaking the truth, especially to those in power, is necessary for the world to be a better place. I've had several jobs where speaking the truth to power ended that career. But doing so also resulted in a better life for individuals and society. Throughout history, those who have spoken the truth have sometimes lost their jobs, been arrested and put in prison, and have even been killed. Those who stay connected to the living source have the courage to speak the truth in love and stand up for what is right. Taking risks may lead to failure in the eyes of others, but God uses imperfect people and their weaknesses to bring about desired changes. That way, God gets the glory, and those who obey God never really fail.

If this book prompts you to know more about the Bible and its messages, consider telling a friend you trust who is a Christian about why you want to know more. Have them suggest other books to read, perhaps a paraphrased version of the Bible, such as the *New Living Translation*. Also consider contacting one or two pastors or priests near you and let them know of your interests and why you contacted them. Ask them what they think are the main messages of the Bible and about the meetings they hold. Consider attending several meetings as a visitor – each gathering has its own "feel" and culture, so see which seems right for you. Collectively, these steps will help you continue your journey and decide what to do next.

APPENDIXES

Appendix A
BOOKS IN THE BIBLE

The number of "chapters" in each book is noted in parentheses.

**Old Testament
(39 Books)**

Genesis (50)
Exodus (40)
Leviticus (27)
Numbers (36)
Deuteronomy (34)
Joshua (24)
Judges (21)
Ruth (4)
1 Samuel (31)
2 Samuel (24)
1 Kings (22)
2 Kings (25)
1 Chronicles (29)
2 Chronicles (36)
Ezra (36)
Nehemiah (13)
Esther (10)
Job (42)
Psalms (150)
Proverbs (31)
Ecclesiastes (12)
Song of Solomon (8)
Isaiah (66)
Jeremiah (52)
Lamentations (5)
Ezekiel (48)
Daniel (12)
Hosea (14)
Joel (3)

Amos (9)
Obadiah (1)
Jonah (4)
Micah (7)
Nahum (3)
Habakkuk (3)
Zephaniah (3)
Haggai (2)
Zechariah (14)
Malachi (4)

**New Testament
(27 Books)**

Matthew (28)
Mark (16)
Luke (24)
John (21)
Acts (28)
Romans (16)
1 Corinthians (16)
2 Corinthians (13)
Galatians (6)
Ephesians (6)
Philippians (4)
Colossians (4)
1 Thessalonians (5)
2 Thessalonians (3)
1 Timothy (6)
2 Timothy (4)
Titus (3)
Philemon (1)
Hebrews (13)
James (5)
1 Peter (5)
2 Peter (3)
1 John (5)
2 John (1)
3 John (1)
Jude (1)
Revelation (22)

APPENDIX B
CHRONOLOGY OF MAIN BIBLICAL
CHARACTERS AND EVENTS
(dates are approximate)

Old Testament	
Prehistory	
• Adam and Eve	Creation of the world
• Noah	Great flood
Patriarchs (1850–1240 BC)	
• Abraham and Sarah	Promises to become God's people
• Isaac and Rebekah	Isaac blesses Jacob
• Esau, Jacob, Rachel, Leah	Jacob leaves then returns to Canaan
• Jacob and his 12 sons	Jacob and his family move to Egypt
• Moses and Aaron	Exodus from Egypt, God gives laws
• Joshua	Israelites enter and occupy Canaan
Judges and Oppressors (1240–1050 BC)	
• Deborah and Barak	Victory over Canaanites in Hazor
• Gideon	Victory over raiders from the east
• Jephthah	Victory over Ammonites
• Samson	Victory over Philistines
• Eli and Samuel	Battles with Philistines
• Boaz and Ruth	Foreigner's child precedes king
Kings (1050–930 BC)	
• Saul	First king of Israel with many flaws
• David	Most famous Israelite hero and king
• Solomon	Wise king expands Israel's territory
Divided Kingdom (930–586 BC)	
• Amos, Elijah, Elisha, Isaiah	People in Northern Kingdom eventually enslaved by the Assyrians (722 BC)
• Isaiah, Micah, Jeremiah	People of Southern Kingdom (Judah) eventually exiled to Babylon
Exile and Return (586–400 BC)	
• Ezekiel and other prophets	Jews settle in Babylonia, many return
• Daniel and Esther	Exiled Jews thrive in Babylonia and Persia
• Ezra and Nehemiah	Jerusalem and the Temple are rebuilt

New Testament

Jesus's Birth and Preparation (5 BC–AD 7)

- Mary, Joseph, and Jesus — God becomes a human
- John the Baptist — Predictions of the Messiah come true

Jesus's Ministry (AD 25–28)

- Twelve disciples — Miracles attract large crowds
- Jewish religious leaders — New ideas challenge existing rules
- Roman political leaders — Jesus is killed but comes back to life

Leaders Spread Good News (28–95)

- Twelve disciples — News about Jesus spreads in Israel
- Saul (Paul) — Good news is extended to Gentiles
- Believers in Asia and Europe — Apostles encourage struggling churches

APPENDIX C
ALIGNMENT WITH BIBLE BOOKS

The chapters of this book provide the main points of the Bible books shown in the table below.

Chapter	Bible Books
1	Genesis, Exodus 1–14
2	Exodus 15–40, Leviticus, Numbers, Deuteronomy, Joshua
3	Judges, Ruth, 1–2 Samuel, 1 Kings, 1–2 Chronicles
4	2 Kings, Amos, Hosea, Isaiah, Micah
5	Jeremiah, Joel, Zephaniah, Obadiah, Nahum, Habakkuk, Lamentations
6	Ezekiel, Daniel, Haggai, Zechariah, Esther, Ezra, Nehemiah, Malachi
7	Proverbs, Ecclesiastes, Job, Jonah, Song of Solomon, Psalms
8	Luke 1–5, John 1, Matthew 1–4
9	Luke 5–10,18–21, John 2–5, Matthew 8–9,11–12,14–15,17
10	Luke 11–21, John 6–9, Matthew 5–7,10–25, Mark
11	Luke 22–24, John 10–21, Matthew 26–28, Acts 1
12	Acts 1–11
13	Acts 12–20
14	Acts 21-28
15	Galatians, 1–2 Thessalonians, 1–2 Corinthians, Romans, Colossians, Ephesians, Philippians, Titus, Philemon, 1–2 Timothy
16	1–2 Peter, James, Jude, 1–3 John, Hebrews
17	Matthew 13,24, Revelation

APPENDIX D
SCRIPTURE VERSES QUOTED

The quoted sections of this book are paraphrases of the scripture verses found in the Old and New Testaments. Most quotes are closest to the New International Version (NIV) of the Bible and are listed in the order they appear in this book.

Chapter	Bible Book, Chapter, Verse		
1	Genesis	12	2–3
1	Genesis	22	12, 17–18
1	Genesis	27	28–29
1	Genesis	45	4–10
1	Exodus	3	4–17
1	Exodus	5	1
2	Exodus	19	3–6
2	Exodus	20	1–17
2	Leviticus	19	18
2	Numbers	14	18
2	Numbers	33	51–53, 55–56
2	Deuteronomy	4	25–27, 29–31
2	Deuteronomy	6	4–5
2	Deuteronomy	9	5–6
3	Judges	16	28
3	Ruth	1	16–17
3	Ruth	2	10–13
3	1 Samuel	1	11
3	1 Samuel	15	22–23
3	1 Samuel	16	7
3	1 Samuel	17	34–36, 45–46
3	2 Samuel	7	9, 12, 16
3	2 Samuel	12	7–11
4	1 Kings	18	27, 36, 39
4	Hosea	12	6
4	Isaiah	1	11, 13, 15–17
4	Isaiah	28	17
4	Isaiah	17	13
4	Isaiah	40	31
4	Isaiah	42	16
4	Isaiah	43	1–2, 19

Chapter Bible Book, Chapter, Verse

Chapter	Bible Book		Verse
4	Isaiah	53	3–5, 7, 9–12
4	Isaiah	58	1–10
4	Isaiah	61	1–3
4	Isaiah	2	2–4
4	Micah	6	8
4	Micah	7	18
5	Jeremiah	1	5, 7–8
5	Nahum	1	3, 7
5	Habakkuk	2	4
6	Jeremiah	29	5–7
6	Ezekiel	36	22–23, 26–27
6	Ezekiel	37	24
6	Daniel	2	27–28, 47
6	Daniel	3	16–18
6	Daniel	6	16, 22
6	Haggai	2	4–7
6	Zechariah	2	4
6	Zechariah	7	9–14
6	Zechariah	8	16, 23
6	Esther	3	8–9
6	Esther	4	16
6	Malachi	3	1–7
7	Proverbs	3	35
7	Ecclesiastes	1	2, 9, 14
7	Job	1	1, 3, 21
7	Job	2	9, 10
7	Job	19	25–26
7	Job	27	4–6
7	Jonah	4	2, 8–11
7	Psalm	1	1–6
8	Luke	1	30–33
8	Matthew	1	20–23
8	Luke	2	10–12, 14
8	Matthew	2	15
8	Luke	2	48–49
8	Matthew	3	2–3
8	Luke	3	4–5, 7–9, 11, 14, 16–17, 22
8	John	1	23, 29
8	Matthew	3	14–15, 17
8	Matthew	4	3–4, 6–10
8	Luke	4	3–4, 6–12

Chapter Bible Book, Chapter, Verse

Chapter	Bible Book		Chapter, Verse
8	Luke	4	18–19, 21, 23–29, 34–35
8	Matthew	4	17
8	Luke	5	5, 8
8	John	1	46
9	John	4	9, 14, 17–18, 23, 26, 29
9	John	3	3–21
9	Luke	18	22–27
9	Luke	19	8–10
9	John	2	4, 10
9	Mark	2	9–11
9	Matthew	9	5–6
9	Luke	7	6–8
9	Matthew	8	10, 13
9	John	5	8
9	Matthew	15	24–28
9	Matthew	8	29, 32
9	Luke	8	28, 30
9	John	11	21, 25–27, 41–43
9	Luke	5	31–32, 34–38
9	John	2	16, 19–20
9	Matthew	14	31
9	Matthew	8	26
9	Luke	10	5
9	Matthew	11	3–5, 10
10	Matthew	15	7–9, 17–20
10	Mark	7	6–8, 15, 18–23
10	Luke	11	39, 41
10	Mark	2	25–27
10	Matthew	12	3–7, 11
10	Luke	6	9
10	Luke	10	27–37
10	Luke	15	4–10, 24, 29–32
10	Matthew	20	15–16
10	Matthew	18	23–34
10	Matthew	13	3–8, 18–23
10	Matthew	5	3–10
10	Matthew	5	11–16, 21–24, 27–30, 38–47
10	Matthew	6	1–4, 19–20, 25–27, 33–34
10	Matthew	7	1–5, 12–27, 7–11
10	Matthew	11	25–30
10	John	8	19, 31–32

Chapter Bible Book, Chapter, Verse

Chapter	Bible Book	Chapter	Verse
10	John	6	32, 35, 37, 53–58, 68–69
10	Matthew	10	37
10	Luke	14	28–31
10	Matthew	10	16–23, 28, 32–33, 39
10	Matthew	25	21, 26–27, 34–45
10	Luke	18	10–14
10	Matthew	21	38, 41–43
10	Mark	12	14–17
11	John	6	35
11	John	11	25
11	John	10	1–18
11	Zechariah	9	9
11	Matthew	21	9
11	John	13	12–15
11	Luke	22	19–20
11	Matthew	26	26–28
11	Mark	10	42–45
11	Matthew	26	2, 31–34
11	John	13	33–35, 37–38
11	John	14	2–12, 16–19, 26
11	John	15	1–8, 18
11	John	16	33
11	Matthew	26	39–42, 45–46, 55–56
11	Matthew	26	63–68, 73
11	Matthew	27	11, 13, 21–23
11	John	19	7
11	Luke	23	21
11	John	19	30
11	Matthew	27	24–25, 40, 42
11	Luke	23	34, 39–43, 46
11	Matthew	27	46
11	Luke	24	7
11	John	20	13–16
11	Luke	24	25–26, 36, 38–39
11	John	20	27–29
11	Luke	24	44–47
11	Matthew	28	18–20
11	John	21	16
11	Acts	1	7–8
12	Acts	2	22–24, 30–32, 36, 38, 40
12	Acts	3	6, 12–16

Chapter Bible Book, Chapter, Verse

Chapter	Bible Book	Chapter	Verse
12	Acts	4	9–12
12	Acts	5	28–31, 36–39
12	Acts	7	56
12	Acts	9	4–6, 15, 17
12	Acts	8	32–33
12	Acts	10	15, 28–29, 34–36, 42–43
12	Acts	11	17
13	Acts	13	46–47
13	Acts	14	11, 15–17
13	Acts	15	7–11, 17
13	Acts	16	17–18, 28, 31
13	Acts	17	22–23
13	Acts	19	13, 15, 28, 34
14	Acts	22	25
14	Acts	23	6, 11
14	Acts	28	26–28
15	Galatians	5	14, 16–23,
15	Galatians	6	1–4, 9–10
15	1 Thess.	4	3, 11–12
15	1 Thess.	5	13–18
15	1 Corinthians	1	27
15	1 Corinthians	3	1–6, 10
15	1 Corinthians	5	9–13
15	1 Corinthians	7	9
15	1 Corinthians	2	16
15	1 Corinthians	9	19–23
15	1 Corinthians	10	13
15	1 Corinthians	14	18–19
15	1 Corinthians	12	16–24, 26
15	1 Corinthians	13	1–13
15	1 Corinthians	15	51–52, 54–55
15	2 Corinthians	12	7, 9
15	Romans	3	11–12, 20, 22–23
15	Romans	5	12–17
15	Romans	8	28, 31, 38
15	Romans	5	3–4, 12, 17
15	Romans	12	2–21
15	Romans	13	1,7
15	Colossians	1	15–20
15	Colossians	2	20–23
15	Colossians	3	5–10, 12–14

Chapter Bible Book, Chapter, Verse

Chapter	Bible Book	Chapter	Verse
15	Colossians	4	5–6
15	Ephesians	2	1–6, 8–9, 11–22
15	Ephesians	5	21–29
15	Ephesians	6	1–9, 12
15	Philippians	2	2–11
15	Philippians	4	6–8, 11–13
15	1 Timothy	6	6–10, 17–19
16	1 Peter	2	9, 20
16	1 Peter	3	3–4, 15
16	1 Peter	4	8
16	1 Peter	5	8–9
16	2 Peter	1	5–8
16	James	1	2–7, 13–17, 22, 26–27
16	James	2	1–4, 8–9, 20–24
16	James	4	4, 13–15
16	James	5	1–5, 16
16	1 John	3	16–18
16	1 John	4	7–8, 18–21
16	Hebrews	1	1–4
16	Hebrews	4	12–15
16	Hebrews	10	24
16	Hebrews	11	1, 3, 8, 11, 13, 16, 26–40
16	Hebrews	12	1–2, 12
17	Matthew	24	6–16, 22–24
17	Matthew	13	24–29
17	Revelation	3	15–17, 19–20
17	Revelation	5	5, 12
17	Revelation	19	6
17	Revelation	21	4–7
17	Revelation	22	12–13, 17, 20
Epilogue	Matthew	28	19–20

APPENDIX E
MAPS

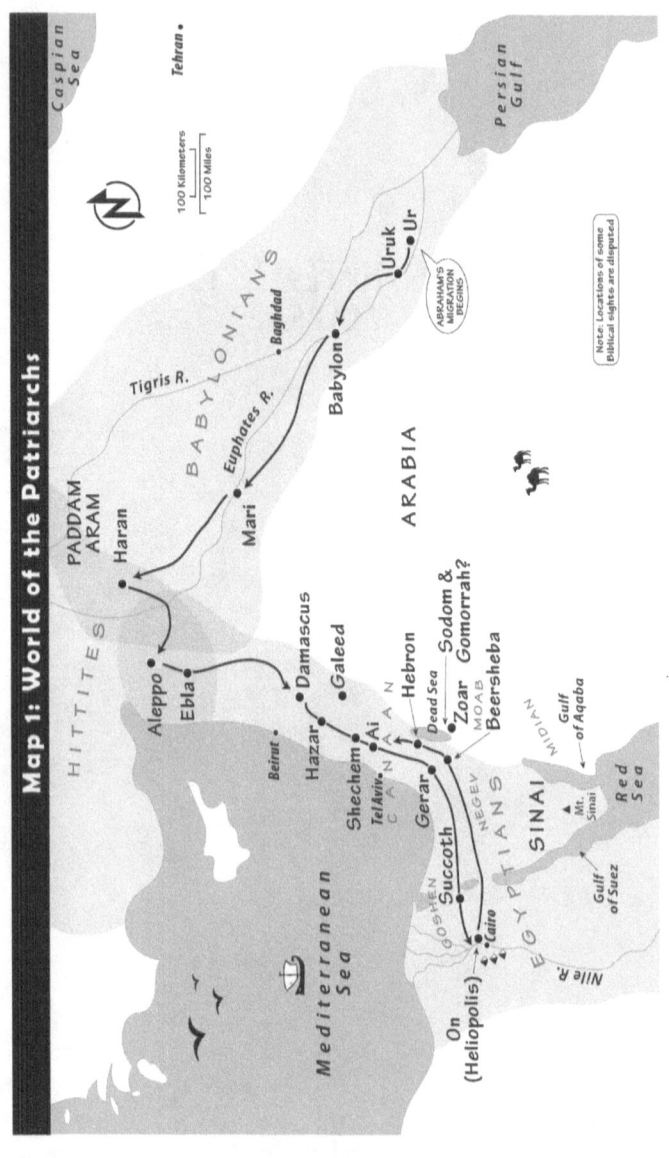

Map 1: World of the Patriarchs

Map 2: Moses & the Exodus

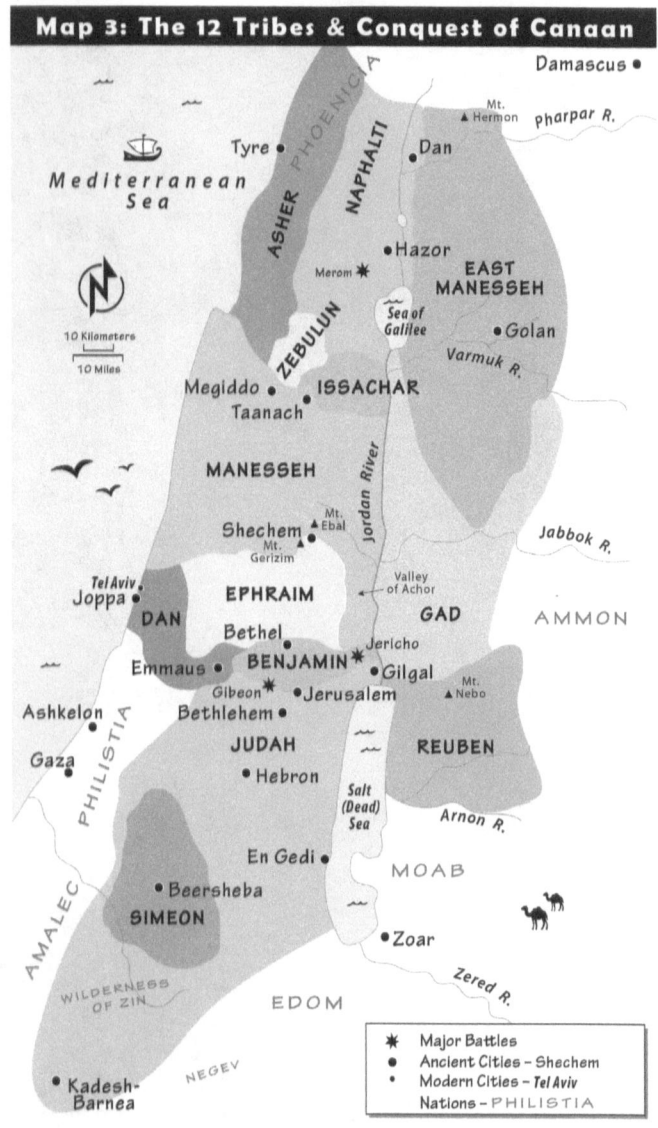

Map 3: The 12 Tribes & Conquest of Canaan

Damascus

PHOENICIA

Mt. Hermon

Pharpar R.

Tyre

ASHER

NAPHALTI

Dan

Mediterranean Sea

Hazor

Merom

EAST MANESSEH

10 Kilometers

10 Miles

ZEBULUN

Sea of Galilee

Golan

Varmuk R.

Megiddo

ISSACHAR

Taanach

MANESSEH

Jordan River

Jabbok R.

Shechem

Mt. Ebal

Mt. Gerizim

Valley of Achor

Tel Aviv

EPHRAIM

GAD

AMMON

Joppa

DAN

Bethel

Jericho

Emmaus

BENJAMIN

Gilgal

Mt. Nebo

Ashkelon

Gibeon

Jerusalem

PHILISTIA

Bethlehem

JUDAH

REUBEN

Gaza

Hebron

Salt (Dead) Sea

Arnon R.

En Gedi

MOAB

AMALEC

Beersheba

SIMEON

Zoar

Zered R.

WILDERNESS OF ZIN

EDOM

NEGEV

Kadesh-Barnea

Major Battles
Ancient Cities – Shechem
Modern Cities – *Tel Aviv*
Nations – PHILISTIA

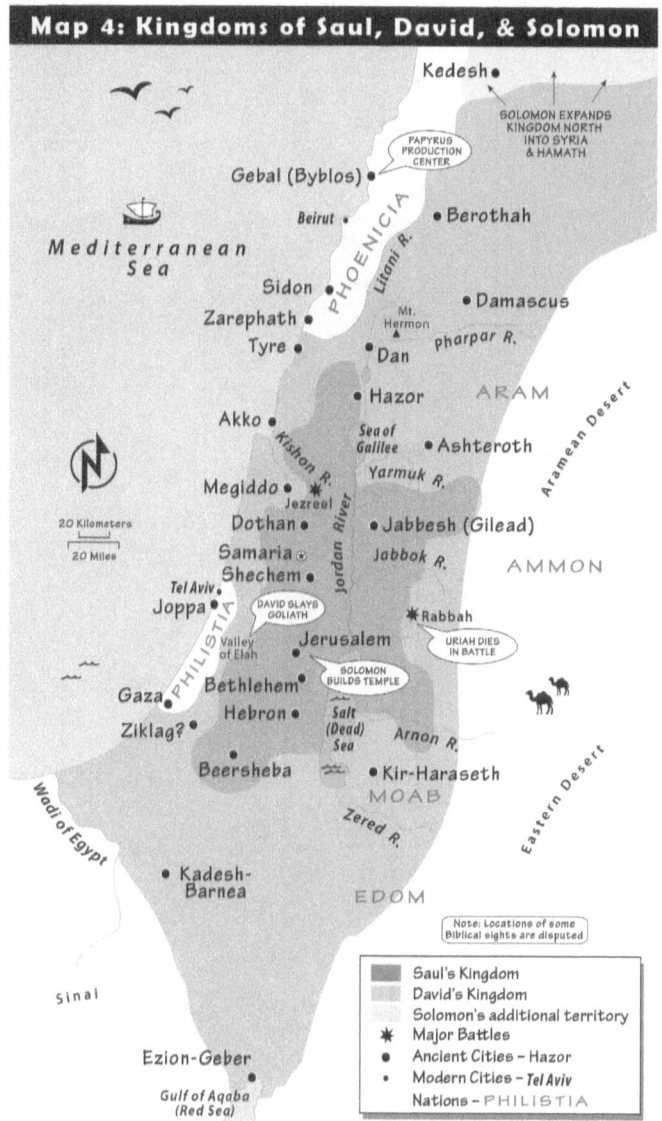

Map 4: Kingdoms of Saul, David, & Solomon

Kedesh •

SOLOMON EXPANDS KINGDOM NORTH INTO SYRIA & HAMATH

PAPYRUS PRODUCTION CENTER

Gebal (Byblos) •

Beirut • PHOENICIA • Berothah

Litani R.

Mediterranean Sea

Sidon •

Zarephath • Mt. Hermon • Damascus

Tyre • pharpar R.

• Dan

• Hazor ARAM

Akko •

Kishon R. Sea of Galilee • Ashteroth Aramean Desert

Megiddo • Yarmuk R.

Jezreel

20 Kilometers

20 Miles

Dothan • Jordan River • Jabbesh (Gilead)

Samaria ⊙ Jabbok R. AMMON

Shechem •

Tel Aviv •

Joppa • DAVID SLAYS GOLIATH

*Rabbah

Valley of Elah Jerusalem • URIAH DIES IN BATTLE

Gaza • PHILISTIA Bethlehem • SOLOMON BUILDS TEMPLE

Ziklag? • Hebron • Salt (Dead) Sea

Arnon R.

Beersheba • ≈ • Kir-Haraseth Eastern Desert

MOAB

Zered R.

Wadi of Egypt

• Kadesh-Barnea EDOM

Note: Locations of some Biblical sights are disputed

Sinai

Ezion-Geber

Gulf of Aqaba (Red Sea)

Legend:

- Saul's Kingdom
- David's Kingdom
- Solomon's additional territory
- ✳ Major Battles
- • Ancient Cities – Hazor
- • Modern Cities – *Tel Aviv*
- Nations – PHILISTIA

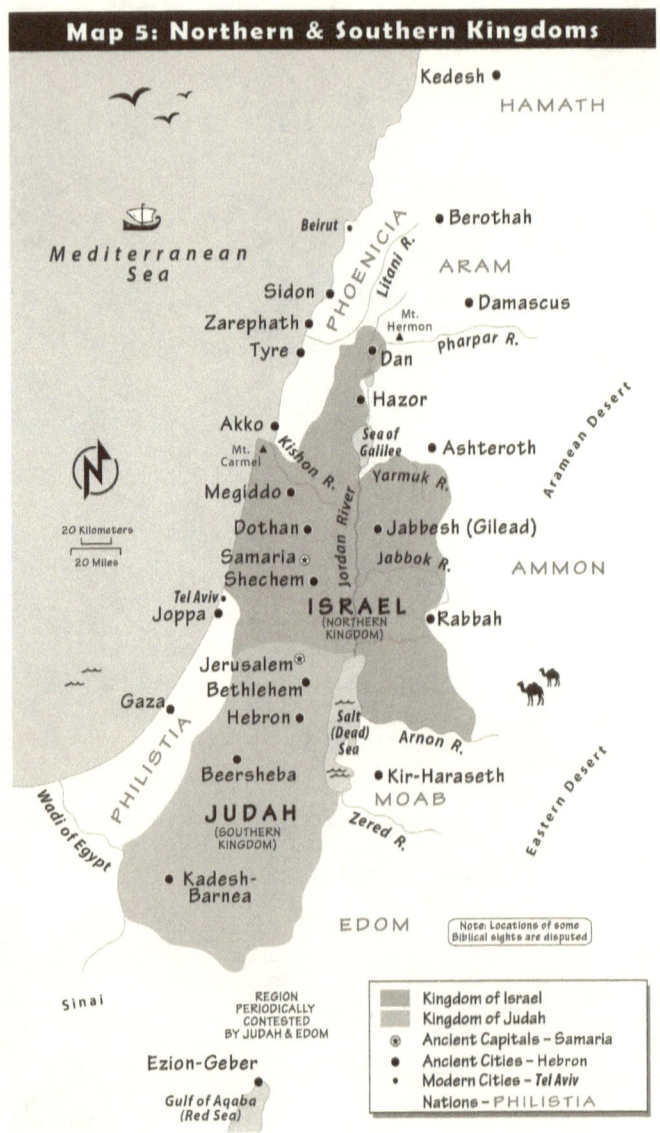

Map 5: Northern & Southern Kingdoms

Kedesh •

HAMATH

Mediterranean Sea

Beirut • • Berothah

PHOENICIA

Litani R.

ARAM

Sidon •

• Damascus

Mt. Hermon ▲

Zarephath •

Pharpar R.

Tyre •

• Dan

• Hazor

Akko •

Sea of Galilee

• Ashteroth

Mt. Carmel ▲

Kishon R.

Aramean Desert

Megiddo •

Yarmuk R.

Dothan •

Jordan River

• Jabbesh (Gilead)

Samaria ⊛

Jabbok R.

Shechem •

AMMON

Tel Aviv •

ISRAEL
(NORTHERN KINGDOM)

Joppa •

• Rabbah

Jerusalem ⊛

Bethlehem •

Gaza •

Hebron •

Salt (Dead) Sea

Arnon R.

PHILISTIA

Beersheba •

• Kir-Haraseth

MOAB

JUDAH
(SOUTHERN KINGDOM)

Zered R.

• Kadesh-Barnea

EDOM

Note: Locations of some
Biblical sights are disputed

Sinai

REGION
PERIODICALLY
CONTESTED
BY JUDAH & EDOM

Wadi of Egypt

Eastern Desert

Ezion-Geber

Gulf of Aqaba
(Red Sea)

20 Kilometers
20 Miles

Kingdom of Israel
Kingdom of Judah
⊛ Ancient Capitals – Samaria
• Ancient Cities – Hebron
• Modern Cities – Tel Aviv
Nations – PHILISTIA

Map 6: Land of the Prophets

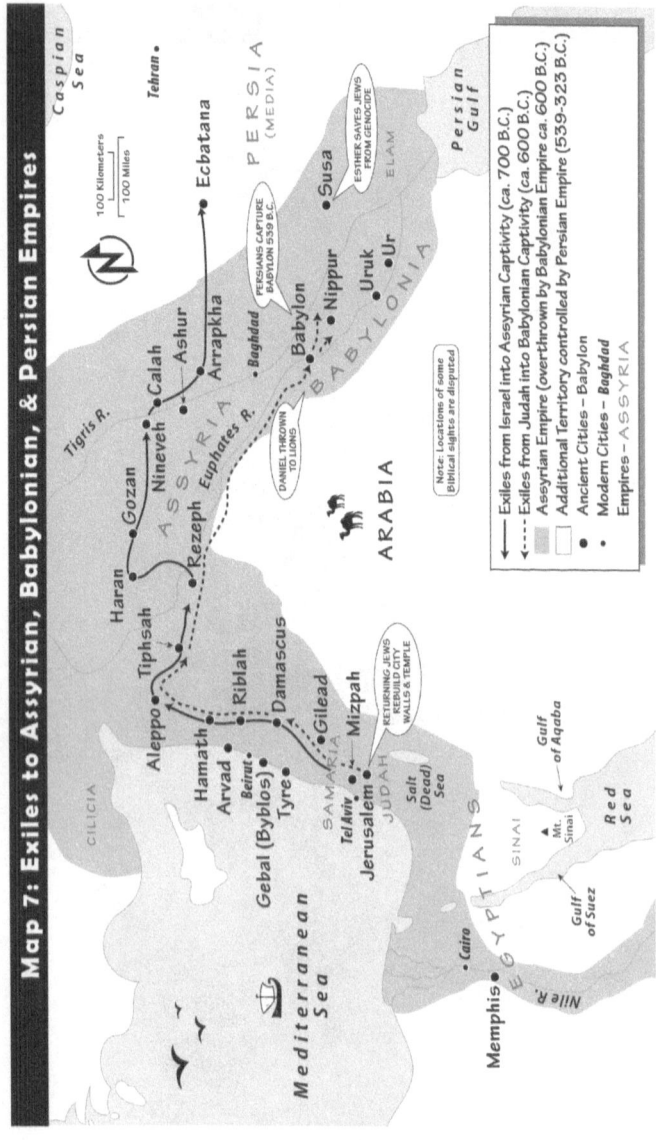

Map 7: Exiles to Assyrian, Babylonian, & Persian Empires

Exiles from Israel into Assyrian Captivity (ca. 700 B.C.)

Exiles from Judah into Babylonian Captivity (ca. 600 B.C.)

Assyrian Empire (overthrown by Babylonian Empire ca. 600 B.C.)

Additional Territory controlled by Persian Empire (539-323 B.C.)

Ancient Cities – Babylon

Modern Cities – *Baghdad*

Empires – ASSYRIA

Note: Locations of some
Biblical sights are disputed

PERSIANS CAPTURE
BABYLON 539 B.C.

DANIEL THROWN
TO LIONS

ESTHER SAVES JEWS
FROM GENOCIDE

RETURNING JEWS
REBUILD CITY
WALLS & TEMPLE

100 Kilometers
100 Miles

*Caspian
Sea*

Tehran

Ecbatana

PERSIA
(MEDIA)

Ashur

Calah

Arrapkha

Baghdad

Babylon

Nippur

Susa

Uruk

Ur

ELAM

BABYLONIA

Persian
Gulf

Nineveh

Gozan

Tigris R.

ASSYRIA

Rezeph

Euphrates R.

Haran

Tiphsah

Aleppo

Hamath

Arvad

Beirut

Gebal (Byblos)

Tyre

Riblah

Damascus

Gilead

Mizpah

SAMARIA

Tel Aviv

Jerusalem

JUDAH

Salt
(Dead)
Sea

CILICIA

*Mediterranean
Sea*

ARABIA

SINAI

Mt.
Sinai

Gulf
of Aqaba

Gulf
of Suez

Cairo

Red
Sea

EGYPTIANS

Nile R.

Memphis

Map 8: Jesus' Ministry in Palestine

10 Kilometers

10 Miles

PHOENICIA

Damascus

HEALS CANAANITE WOMAN'S DAUGHTER

Mt. Hermon ▲

pharpar R.

Tyre

Caesarea Philippi

Mediterranean Sea

MEETS FIRST DISCIPLES, HEALS PARALYZED MEN

SERMON ON THE MOUNT?

HEALS BLIND MAN

Chorazin

Bethsaida

TURNS WATER INTO WINE

Capernaum

Cana

Gerasa

GALILEE

Sea of Galilee

CASTS OUT DEMONS

Nazareth

▲ Mt. Tabor

BOYHOOD

WALKS ON WATER

RAISES MAN FROM DEAD

Nain

Caesarea

SAMARIA

PEREA

DECAPOLIS

Sychar ▲ Mt. Ebal

Jabbok R.

Tel Aviv

SPEAKS WITH SAMARITAN WOMAN AT WELL

▲ Mt. Gerizim

TEMPTATION BY SATAN IN WILDERNESS?

Joppa

Jordan River

APPEARS AFTER RESURRECTION

Bethel

BAPTIZED BY JOHN? (TRADITIONAL)

Emmaus

Mount of Olives

Jerusalem

Bethany

▲ Mt. Nebo

Ashkelon

Bethlehem

BIRTHPLACE

RAISES LAZARUS FROM DEAD

Gaza

JUDEA

LAST SUPPER, CRUCIFIXION

Hebron

Arnon R.

Salt (Dead) Sea

Masada

Beersheba

Zered R.

Note: Locations of some Biblical sights are disputed

To Egypt

Kadesh-Barnea

● Ancient Cities – Sychar
· Modern Cities – Tel Aviv
Nations – PHOENICIA

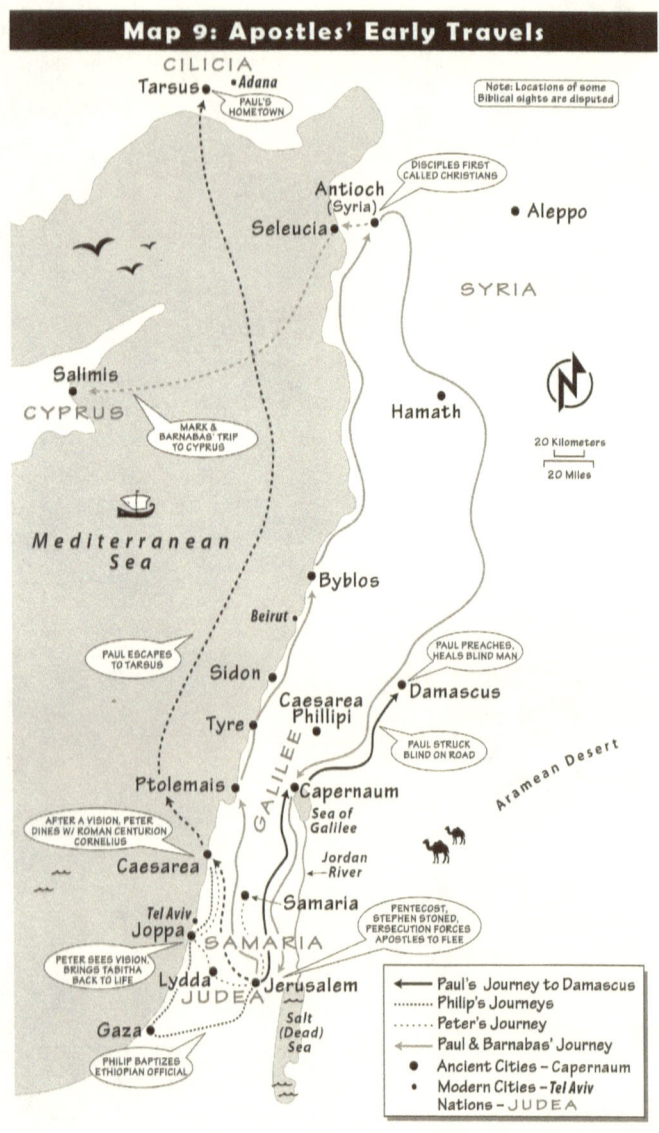

Map 9: Apostles' Early Travels

CILICIA

Tarsus • •Adana
PAUL'S HOMETOWN

Note: Locations of some Biblical sights are disputed

DISCIPLES FIRST CALLED CHRISTIANS

Antioch (Syria)

Seleucia •

• Aleppo

SYRIA

Salimis

CYPRUS

MARK & BARNABAS' TRIP TO CYPRUS

Hamath •

20 Kilometers
20 Miles

Mediterranean Sea

• Byblos

Beirut •

PAUL PREACHES, HEALS BLIND MAN

PAUL ESCAPES TO TARSUS

Sidon •

Caesarea Phillipi

• Damascus

Tyre •

PAUL STRUCK BLIND ON ROAD

Aramean Desert

Ptolemais •

GALILEE

• Capernaum

Sea of Galilee

AFTER A VISION, PETER DINES W/ ROMAN CENTURION CORNELIUS

Jordan River

Caesarea •

Tel Aviv

Joppa •

• Samaria

PENTECOST, STEPHEN STONED, PERSECUTION FORCES APOSTLES TO FLEE

PETER SEES VISION, BRINGS TABITHA BACK TO LIFE

SAMARIA

Lydda • • Jerusalem

JUDEA

Salt (Dead) Sea

Gaza •

PHILIP BAPTIZES ETHIOPIAN OFFICIAL

⟵ Paul's Journey to Damascus
········· Philip's Journeys
·········· Peter's Journey
⟵ Paul & Barnabas' Journey
• Ancient Cities – Capernaum
• Modern Cities – *Tel Aviv*
Nations – JUDEA

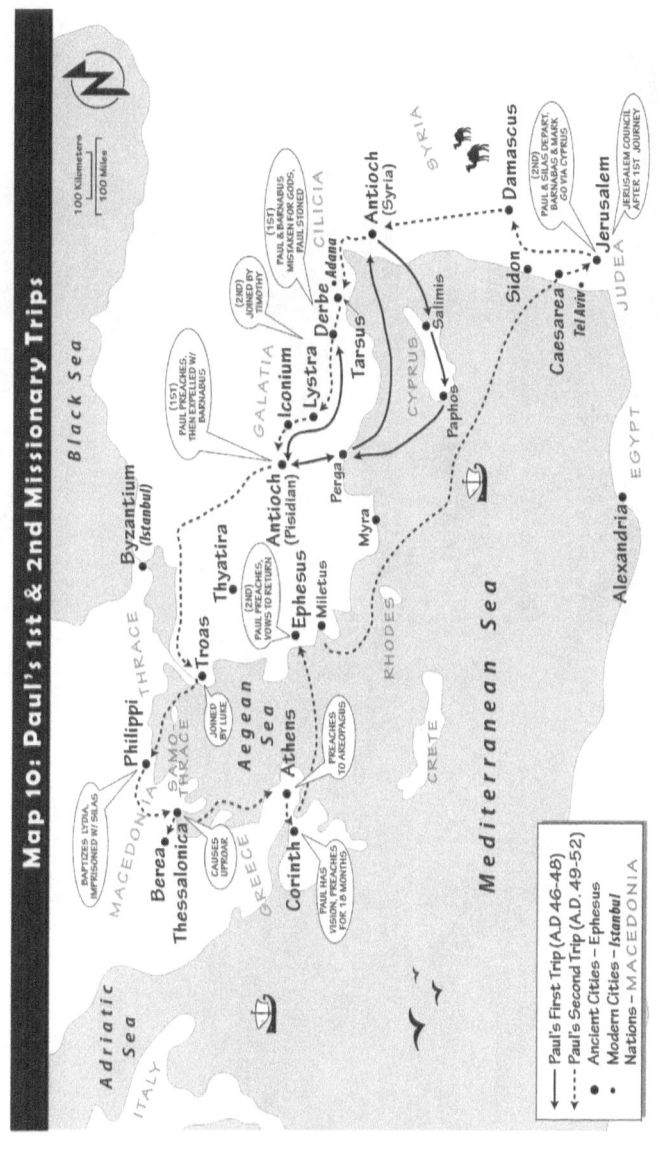

Map 10: Paul's 1st & 2nd Missionary Trips

100 Kilometers
100 Miles

N

Black Sea

Byzantium
(Istanbul)

THRACE

Philippi

SAMO-
THRACE

MACEDONIA

Troas

Thyatira

Aegean
Sea

Berea

Thessalonica

GREECE

Athens

Corinth

CRETE

Ephesus

Miletus

RHODES

Mediterranean
Sea

Antioch
(Pisidian)

Perga

Myra

GALATIA

Iconium

Lystra

Derbe

Adana

Tarsus

CILICIA

Antioch
(Syria)

SYRIA

Damascus

CYPRUS

Salimis

Paphos

Sidon

Caesarea

Tel Aviv

Jerusalem

JUDEA

EGYPT

Alexandria

Adriatic
Sea

ITALY

BAPTIZES LYDIA, IMPRISONED W/ SILAS

JOINED BY LUKE

CAUSES UPROAR

PAUL HAS VISION, PREACHES FOR 18 MONTHS

PREACHES TO AREOPAGUS

(2ND) PAUL PREACHES, VOWS TO RETURN

(1ST) PAUL PREACHES, THEN EXPELLED W/ BARNABAS

(2ND) JOINED BY TIMOTHY

(1ST) PAUL & BARNABAS MISTAKEN FOR GODS, PAUL STONED

(2ND) PAUL & SILAS DEPART, BARNABAS & MARK GO VIA CYPRUS

JERUSALEM COUNCIL AFTER 1ST JOURNEY

→ Paul's First Trip (A.D. 46-48)
• • • Paul's Second Trip (A.D. 49-52)
• Ancient Cities — Ephesus
• Modern Cities — *Istanbul*
Nations — MACEDONIA

225

Maps

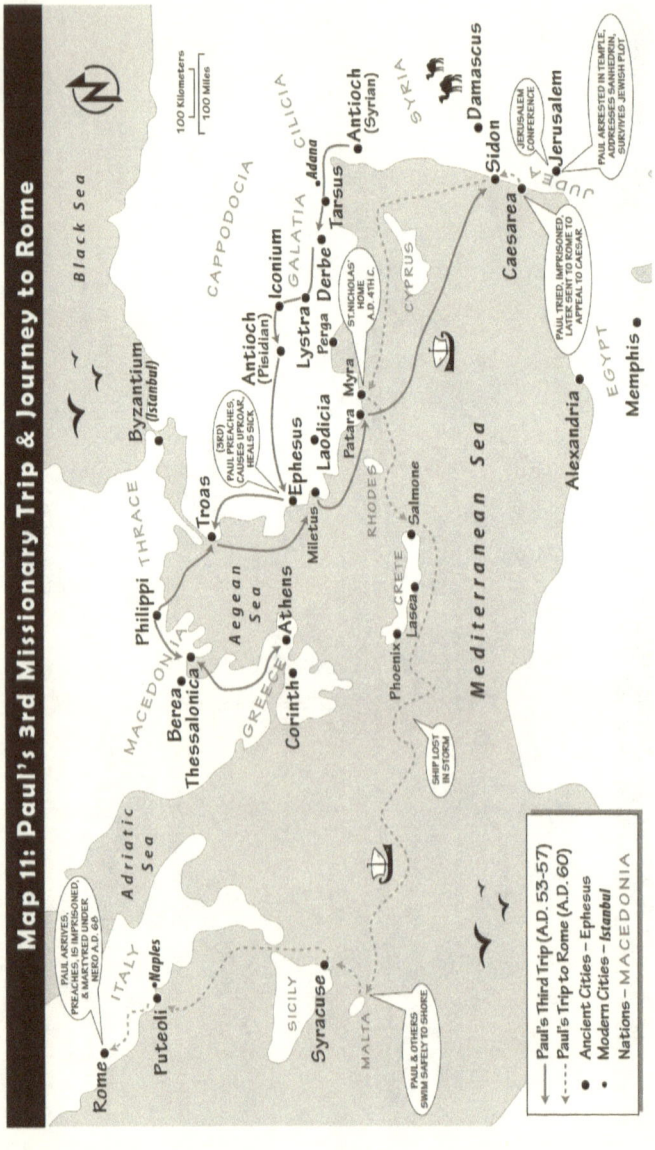

226

About the Author

Peter J. Bylsma earned a bachelor's degree in psychology *magna cum laude* from Wheaton College (IL) as well as a master's degree in public administration and a doctorate in education leadership and policy from the University of Washington (Seattle). Dr. Bylsma served 10 years in Christian agencies before working 30 years in public service positions at the international, national, state, and local levels. He has researched many topics in an objective manner and summarized the issues for busy people. He has lived in seven states and four other countries and now lives with his wife in the Puget Sound region of Washington state.

Dr. Bylsma is the author of *The Short Bible* and its related versions in English and other languages, and is the President of the Bylsma Foundation and Byblio Press. Information about the author, his books, and the Foundation is available at *www.bylsmafoundation.org.*